CONTENTS

NOTES ON EDITORS AND CONTRIBUTORS

ALAN BADDELEY is Director of the Medical Research Council Applied Psychology Unit in Cambridge, and Professor of Cognitive Psychology at Cambridge University. He previously taught at the universities of Sussex and Stirling, and has been president of the Experimental Psychology Society and the European Society for Cognitive Psychology. His books include *The Psychology of Memory* (1976), *Your Memory: A User's Guide* (1982), *Working Memory* (1986), and *Human Memory: Theory and Practice* (1990).

ANDREW M. COLMAN is Reader in Psychology at the University of Leicester, having previously taught at Rhodes and Cape Town Universities in South Africa. He is the founder and former editor of the journal *Current Psychology* and Chief Examiner for the British Psychological Society's Qualifying Examination. His books include *Facts, Fallacies and Frauds in Psychology* (1987), *What is Psychology? The Inside Story* (2nd edn, 1988), and *Game Theory and its Applications in the Social and Biological Sciences* (2nd edn, 1995).

JONATHAN St B. T. EVANS is Professor of Cognitive Psychology at the University of the South West in Plymouth. Since completing his doctorate at University College London in 1972, he has researched and published extensively in the psychology of human reasoning and judgement with particular emphasis on the study of biases. He is author of three books on human reasoning, including *Bias in Human Reasoning: Causes and Consequences* (1989); and (with others) *Human Reasoning: The Psychology of Deduction*.

MICHAEL W. EYSENCK is Professor of Psychology and Head of Department at Royal Holloway and Bedford New College, University of London, at Egham, Surrey. He has been Visiting Professor at the University of South Florida. He was the founding editor of the *European Journal of Cognitive Psychology*. He has published approximately 80 articles and book chapters, mainly in the area of anxiety and cognition. He is the author of 18 books,

COGNITIVE PSYCHOLOGY

Longman Essential Psychology
Series editor: Andrew M. Colman

including *Attention and Arousal: Cognition and Performance* (1982) and *Anxiety: The Cognitive Perspective* (1992); he is co-author (with M. T. Keane) of *Cognitive Psychology: A Student's Handbook* (1990).

CHRISTOPHER C. FRENCH is Senior Lecturer in Psychology at Goldsmiths' College, University of London. His two main research interests at the present time are the relationship between cognition and emotion, and cognitive factors underlying paranormal beliefs. He has published papers on these and a variety of other topics including human cerebral asymmetry, computerised psychometric assessment, peace psychology, and everyday memory. He is the co-author, with Herbert H. Blumberg, of *The Persian Gulf War: Views From the Social and Behavioral Sciences* (1994).

ALAN GARNHAM read Psychology, Philosophy, and Physiology at Oxford University before obtaining a DPhil in Experimental Psychology from Sussex University. He has since worked as a Research Fellow at Sussex University and as a Lecturer at Reading and Sussex Universities. His principal research interests are in psycholinguistics; he is currently engaged in research on the interpretation of anaphoric expressions and on syntactic analysis and ambiguity. In addition to publishing numerous journal articles and book chapters, he is the author of *Psycholinguistics: Central Topics* (1985), *Mental Models as Representations of Discourse and Text* (1987), *Artificial Intelligence: An Introduction* (1988), *The Mind in Action* (1991), and co-author (with Jane Oakhill) of *Becoming a Skilled Reader* (1988).

WILLEM J. M. LEVELT is Director of the Max Planck Institute for Psycholinguistics, Nijmegen, The Netherlands, and Professor of Psycholinguistics at Nijmegen University. He is author of *On Binocular Rivalry* (1968), *Formal Grammars in Linguistics and Psycholinguistics* (three volumes, 1974), and *Speaking: From Intention to Articulation* (1989).

SERIES EDITOR'S PREFACE

The *Longman Essential Psychology* series comprises twelve concise and inexpensive paperback volumes covering all of the major topics studied in undergraduate psychology degree courses. The series is intended chiefly for students of psychology and other subjects with psychology components, including medicine, nursing, sociology, social work, and education. Each volume contains five or six accessibly written chapters by acknowledged authorities in their fields, and each chapter includes a list of references and a small number of recommendations for further reading.

Most of the material was prepared originally for the Routledge *Companion Encyclopedia of Psychology* but with a view to later paperback subdivision – the contributors were asked to keep future textbook readers at the front of their minds. Additional material has been added for the paperback series: new co-editors have been recruited for nine of the volumes that deal with highly specialized topics, and each volume has a new introduction, a glossary of technical terms including a number of entries written specially for this edition, and a comprehensive new index.

I am grateful to my literary agents Sheila Watson and Amanda Little for clearing a path through difficult terrain towards the publication of this series, to Sarah Caro of Longman for her patient and efficient preparation of the series, to Brian Parkinson, David Stretch, and Susan Dye for useful advice and comments, and to Carolyn Preston for helping with the compilation of the glossaries.

ANDREW M. COLMAN

INTRODUCTION

Christopher C. French
Goldsmiths' College, University of London, England

Andrew M. Colman
University of Leicester, England

Many contemporary psychologists would describe themselves as cognitive psychologists. This reflects not only the fact that cognitive psychology is currently the dominant approach within academic psychology, but also the increasing vagueness of the term *cognitive*. After all, if the cognitive approach is seen to dominate, it is not surprising that many different types of psychologists want to identify themselves with it. However, it is probably fair to say that mainstream cognitive psychology is most closely related to what used to be called *experimental psychology*. In this volume, four of the five chapters deal with core components of mainstream cognitive psychology – memory, attention, psycholinguistics, thinking, and reasoning – largely from the perspective of human experimental psychology. The final chapter discusses various cognitive topics from the particular perspective of artificial intelligence which, along with experimental studies of cognition in normal humans and the neuropsychological approach, constitutes one of the main approaches within cognitive psychology.

The word *cognition* comes from the Latin *cognoscere*, which means to apprehend. According to *Chambers English Dictionary*, to apprehend means to be conscious of by the senses; to lay hold of by the intellect; to catch the meaning of; understand; to recognize; to consider. These meanings are all covered in the following chapters. Increasingly, however, it is recognized that cognitive psychologists must take into account the effects of motivation, emotion, and a range of other psychological factors. So why not just say that cognitive psychology is synonymous with psychology as a whole? The main reason is that cognitive psychology is characterized by a particular approach to its subject matter: the information-processing approach.

The information-processing approach views mental events in terms of information flow. It implies a somewhat mechanistic view of the mind, which is seen as being enormously flexible and adaptive but nevertheless as a rule-governed automaton. Information-processing models of cognitive processes are often represented as flowcharts (for example, Figure 1 of chapter 1). Flowcharts highlight the often implicit assumption that mental operations occur in a clear sequence. Early cognitive models tended to assume that each component (each of the boxes in the flowcharts) had to complete its processing before passing on the results to the next component (via the arrows). This *serial processing* assumption is increasingly questioned and contrasted with *parallel processing* models (for example, connectionist models, see chapter 5).

Early cognitive theories also tended to assume that stimuli impinge on a passive organism and are processed in a fairly automatic manner. In fact it is easy to demonstrate that the expectations of the organism influence what is perceived and remembered. This is an example of what is known as a *top-down* influence on processing (because it originates at a "higher" level within the cognitive system), in contrast to the *stimulus-driven* or *bottom-up* influences emphasized by early theories. Cognitive processes often involve complex interplays of both top-down and bottom-up processes. At the heart of cognitive psychology is the notion that cognition involves processes acting on and transforming symbolic representations in ways that allow the organism to model the external world internally. This internal model is based on the interaction between stimulus information from the senses and what we already believe about the way the world operates.

The cognitive approach may legitimately be applied to other traditional subdivisions within psychology. With respect to developmental psychology, for example, we can ask questions regarding how cognitive processes change, for better or for worse, with ageing. We can also ask how cognitive representations of the world develop during childhood and how this relates to children's behaviour and abilities. Indeed, the approach of Piaget, one of the founders of developmental psychology as we know it today, was very much in the spirit of modern cognitive psychology. In social psychology, topics such as social interaction, attitude formation, and belief systems, to name but a few, are often approached from an information-processing perspective.

Recently, ideas from mainstream cognitive psychology have been applied with considerable success in attempts to understand the traditional subject matter of abnormal psychology, such as anxiety and depression. It has been shown, for example, that anxiety and depression both influence cognitive processing but in surprisingly different ways (Mathews & MacLeod, 1994). It is appropriate at this point, however, to emphasize that many clinicians

COGNI ... OLOGY

Christopher C. French
and
Andrew M. Colman

Longman Group Limited
Longman House, Burnt Mill
Harlow, Essex CM20 2JE, England
and Associated Companies throughout the world.

Published in the United States of America
by Longman Publishing, New York

© 1994 Routledge
This edition © 1995 Longman Group Limited
Compilation © 1995 Andrew Colman

This edition first published 1995

ISBN 0 582 27810 4 PPR

British Library Cataloguing-in-Publication Data
A catalogue record for this book is available from the British Library.

Library of Congress Cataloging-in-Publication Data
A catalogue record for this book is available from the Library of Congress.

Typeset by 25 in 10/12pt Times
Printed and bound by Bookcraft (Bath) Ltd

who refer to themselves as cognitive therapists actually do very little that corresponds in any way to the activities of mainstream experimental cognitive psychologists. This is an example of the vagueness, referred to earlier, of the term cognitive.

The relationship between cognitive psychology and neuropsychology is so important that it merits special mention. In recent years, the relationship between the two has led to the establishment of the field of *cognitive neuropsychology*. Alongside human experimental psychology and artificial intelligence, cognitive neuropsychology is one of the three main approaches to cognition. Cognitive neuropsychology is concerned with the patterns of normal and impaired functioning in brain-damaged patients. This can provide an extremely useful way to test cognitive theories. One of the most fruitful examples of this approach is in terms of cognitive models of reading and writing. By studying the particular pattern of errors made by a brain-damaged patient and contrasting it with the patterns of errors made by other patients, the validity of different models of reading and writing can be tested. It is assumed, for example, that different routes exist for translating written words into speech (see chapter 3). Some brain-damaged patients seem able to read only by translating each letter into its corresponding sound. These patients have great difficulty reading orthographically irregular words such as "yacht". Others seem to have the ability to read only via whole word recognition, and they have great difficulty reading simple non-words such as "bink" because they cannot translate letters into sounds. Such observations offer clear support for the existence of more than one route from the printed to the spoken word (Ellis, 1993). *Ref to Chapter III*

It is important to be aware of the limitations of neuropsychological data in providing explanations of normal cognition. Cognitive neuropsychologists often assume that the cognitive system is basically modular, that is, that it consists of numerous relatively independent cognitive processing subsystems. Brain damage typically affects the functioning of some (but not all) of these subsystems, and so it should ultimately be possible to use data gathered by studying brain-damaged patients to specify the number and nature of cognitive subsystems. In practice, brain damage is often fairly extensive, and this complicates the enterprise. Little can be deduced if a patient shows general impairments across a wide range of tasks. Furthermore, brain-damaged patients may use different strategies from those used by other people to perform a task, and this must also be taken into account. In spite of all these problems, such data remain amongst the most useful in cognitive psychology.

In computer science, the term *computation* refers not just to numerical calculation (addition, multiplication, and so on) but more generally to symbol manipulation. The computer seems to offer a particularly appropriate analogy for human cognition. Both computers and people take in information, process it in a number of ways, and produce various types of output. It therefore seems natural that psychologists should use computers to try to simulate human cognition. Computer simulation is not synonymous with artificial intelligence or AI (see chapter 5). AI is concerned with making computers perform tasks that we would normally think of as requiring intelligence, whereas computer simulation has the rather more specific aim of making computers perform such tasks in the same way that humans do. Naturally, this requires a psychological theory as a starting point. If a theory of cognitive performance is precise and explicit enough, it can be implemented on a computer. If the computer performs in the same way as a human being, including making the same errors, this provides good support for the model – although it does not, of course, prove that the model is correct.

As well as being part of psychology as a whole, cognitive psychology is also part of the more general interdisciplinary subject of cognitive science. The other major disciplines involved, in addition to neuropsychology and computer science, are linguistics and philosophy. These other disciplines have had a major influence on cognitive psychology and vice versa. Behaviourism, the dominant approach within psychology before the rise of cognitive psychology, was shown to be unable to explain the acquisition and use of language. The field of linguistics was revolutionized by Noam Chomsky's ideas, and Chomsky was very influential in attacking simplistic behaviourist explanations of language behaviour. Philosophical issues such as the nature of mind and consciousness have taxed great thinkers for centuries. Clearly, such issues cannot be avoided in cognitive psychology (see chapter 5 for a discussion of some philosophical issues raised by artificial intelligence).

The five chapters in this volume cover core topics of cognitive psychology, and inevitably there is some overlap between their contents. In chapter 1, which deals with memory, Alan Baddeley distinguishes between sensory memory, working memory, and long-term memory, which have quite distinct properties and functions, and he discusses at some length the real-world implications of the major research findings on working memory and long-term memory in particular. Among the issues he deals with are the unreliability of eyewitness testimony, prospective memory (remembering to do things), and autobiographical memory (remembering things that have happened in the past). He concludes with some brief comments on the psychoanalytic (Freudian) theory of forgetting as repression. For further discussion of memory see the suggestions for further reading at the end of chapter 1 and also the books by Parkin (1993) and Cohen, Kiss, and Le Voi (1993).

In chapter 2, Michael W. Eysenck provides a general overview of the psychology of attention, including focused attention and visual attention (attending to an auditory or visual message that is accompanied by distracting signals). This chapter also deals with research into divided attention, absent-mindedness, and vigilance (sustained attention during prolonged, monotonous tasks, such as watching a radar screen for occasional unexpected blips, or proof-reading a book looking for typographical errors). Eysenck's discussion of absent-mindedness, in particular, intersects with Baddeley's remarks on the fallibility of memory in chapter 1. For more information on attention, see Eysenck's suggestions for further reading.

Willem J. M. Levelt's survey of psycholinguistics in chapter 3 covers all of the main areas of research into the psychology of language apart from language acquisition. Chapter 3 deals with both speech production and the understanding of speech, and it contains additional material on reading and sign language. Some of these topics are also considered in chapter 5 in relation to artificial intelligence. Levelt's suggestions for further reading will be helpful to readers who wish to pursue psycholinguistics in greater depth.

In chapter 4 Jonathan St B. T. Evans discusses thinking and reasoning. With the help of some fascinating logical puzzles that have been used in experimental investigations, Evans summarizes what is known about problem solving, reasoning, and subjective judgements of probability. For more information on thinking and reasoning, in addition to the suggestions for further reading at the end of chapter 4, see Kahney (1993), and Garnham and Oakhill (1994). For highly readable accounts of the ways in which the fallibility of human reasoning can have effects in everyday life, see Sutherland (1992). Topics considered in chapters 1 to 4 of the current volume are also dealt with by Smyth, Collins, Morris and Levy (1994).

Finally, in chapter 5, Alan Garnham discusses certain aspects of thinking, reasoning, and problem solving, from the slightly different perspective of artificial intelligence. Other topics considered from this perspective include knowledge representation, vision, language, and learning. The history of the discipline is also considered, as are applications and philosophical issues. The suggestions for further reading at the end of chapter 5 contain further information on artificial intelligence. For more detail on connectionism, see Bechtel and Abrahamsen (1991), and for a consideration of the philosophical issues raised by artificial intelligence, see Copeland (1993).

REFERENCES

Bechtel, W., & Abrahamsen, A. (1991). *Connectionism and the mind: An introduction to parallel processing in networks.* Oxford: Blackwell.

Cohen, G., Kiss, G., & Le Voi, M. (1993). *Memory: Current issues* (2nd edn.). Milton Keynes: Open University Press.

Copeland, J. (1993). *Artificial intelligence: A philosophical introduction.* Oxford: Blackwell.

Ellis, A. W. (1993). *Reading writing and dyslexia: A cognitive analysis* (2nd edn.). London: Erlbaum.

Garnham, A., & Oakhill, J. (1994). *Thinking and reasoning.* Oxford: Blackwell.

Kahney, H. (1993). *Problem solving: Current issues* (2nd edn.). Milton Keynes: Open University Press.

Mathews, A., & MacLeod, C. (1994). Cognitive approaches to emotion and emotional disorders. *Annual Review of Psychology.* 45, 25–50.

Parkin, A. (1993). *Memory: Phenomena, experiment and theory*. Oxford: Blackwell.

Smyth, M. M., Collins, A. F., Morris, P. E., & Levy, P. (1994). *Cognition in action* (2nd. edn.). Hove: Erlbaum.

Sutherland, S. (1992). *Irrationality: The enemy within*. London: Constable.

1

MEMORY

Alan Baddeley

MRC Applied Psychology Unit, Cambridge, England

No one would deny that memory is a faculty of some importance, but just how important? Perhaps the best way of gaining some insight into this is to consider the case of patients who have had the misfortune to become amnesic following brain damage. Any loss of neural tissue will tend to be reflected in slower learning and recall, but certain deficits can have an effect that is quite catastrophic. This was dramatically illustrated in a TV programme made by Jonathan Miller (1986) about Clive Wearing, a very intelligent and cultured musician who became densely amnesic following encephalitis, a brain infection caused by the herpes simplex virus. Clive's illness meant that he was left with a desperately impaired capacity to remember new and ongoing information. Since he could not remember anything from more than a minute or two before, he was perpetually convinced that he had just recovered consciousness. A typical remark would be "Consciousness has come to light since I was standing there . . . I was blind, deaf and dumb . . . everything has suddenly come back". He was found on occasion with a notebook in front of him containing the statement "Have just recovered consciousness 3.15 pm", with 3.15 crossed out and changed to 3.20, 3.25, and so forth. If his wife left the room for five minutes, on her return he would greet her as if he had not seen her for months, asking how long it was that he had been

1

unconscious. In short, he lived in a perpetual present, which he described as "like being dead – all the bloody time!"

He had rather better access to memories that occurred before his illness, but even here his memory was far from good. He had written a book on the early composer Lassus, and could answer a few very general questions on him, but could provide virtually no detail. When shown pictures of Cambridge where he had spent four years, he failed to recognize any of the scenes other than King's College Chapel. His general knowledge was likewise impoverished; he could not recall who had written *Romeo and Juliet*, although he could still talk in a lively and intelligent way on more general issues, such as for example the development of the role of the conductor in early music.

Amidst this desert of impaired memory, one capacity was marvellously preserved, namely his musical skills. His wife returned home one evening to find that he had been visited by his choir, and to see him conducting them with all his old skill through a complex choral piece. He could play the harpsichord and sing and to all intents and purposes appeared to have retained his marvellous musical facility. Despite this, however, his grossly impaired access to his own long-term past, and his incapacity to develop and build up an ongoing picture of experience make life for him "a living hell". A few minutes with Clive is enough to convince one of the enormous importance of memory. We all tend to complain that our memories are terrible; what follows aims to persuade you that far from being terrible the human memory system is superb, although fallible.

MEMORY SYSTEMS

We have so far discussed human memory as if it were a single entity like the lungs or heart. It is much better considered as an alliance of several different systems, all of which have in common the capacity to take in information, store it, and subsequently make it available. We shall begin by suggesting that memory can be divided into three broad categories: *sensory memory, working memory,* and *long-term memory*. A diagram illustrating the relationship between the three is shown in Figure 1. Information is assumed to initially be taken up by a series of sensory memory systems, shown on the left of Figure 1. These are perhaps best considered as part of the processes of perception, and include a brief visual memory system sometimes known as *iconic memory*, and its auditory equivalent *echoic memory*. Little more will be said about them here other than that they play an integral part in our perception of the world. For example, if we had no iconic memory system we would perceive a film at the cinema as a series of still images interspersed with blank intervals, rather than as a continuously moving scene. Similarly, without echoic memory we would not hear a word, or indeed even a single tone as an entity. However, such systems probably do not play an important

2

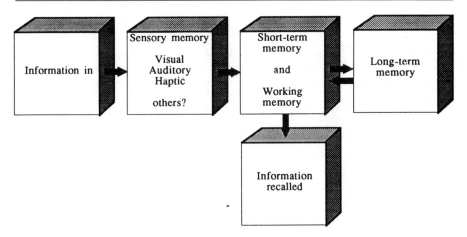

Figure 1 The flow of information through the memory system
Source: Adapted from Atkinson and Shiffrin, 1971

role in those aspects of memory that will concern the rest of this account, and for that reason we shall now move on to talk about working memory.

Working memory

Suppose you were asked to multiply 27 by 9. In order to perform this task by the usual method you need to remember the 27, multiply the 7 by the 9, remember the 3, carry the 6, and so on, eventually coming up with the solution. In reaching that solution you will have to remember small amounts of information for short periods of time, subsequently discarding that information as it ceases to be useful. The system that performs this task of temporarily manipulating information is typically termed *working memory*. It is itself far from unitary, and Figure 2 shows one conceptualization of the structure of working memory.

Working memory is assumed to comprise an attentional coordinating system known as the *Central Executive* aided by a number of subsidiary slave systems of which two are illustrated, namely the *Visuo-spatial Sketchpad*, which is used for setting up and manipulating visual images, and the *Articulatory Loop*, a system that holds and utilizes inner speech.

Some feel for the operation of one's working memory can be gained from attempting the task of working out how many windows there are in your present home. Try it.

Most people attempt to do this task by forming a visual image of their house and then counting the windows either by imagining looking from outside or walking through the house. The Visuo-spatial Sketchpad is the system used for setting up and manipulating the image, the Articulatory Loop is

3

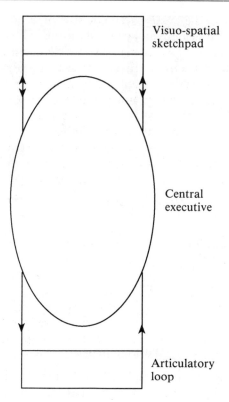

Visuo-spatial
sketchpad

Central
executive

Articulatory
loop

Figure 2   A simplified representation of the working memory model

involved in the process of subvocal counting, while the whole strategy is
organized and run by the Central Executive.

The system has been explored over the years using a number of
approaches, including that of using a specific task to interfere with a particular part of the system. For example, a visuo-spatial task such as steering a
car will interfere with the operation of the sketchpad, and vice versa. A particularly clear example of this occurred when I attempted to drive a car along
an American freeway at the same time as listening to an American football
game on the radio. As I formed a more and more precise image of the game
and its state, I found that the car weaved from side to side because of the
interference between the two uses of my sketchpad. I hurriedly switched to
a music programme.

A rather intriguing example of the use of the sketchpad came from a study
of Japanese abacus experts. In Japan the use of the abacus for mental calculation is common, and practitioners become extremely skilled. With sufficient
practice, the expert learns to dispense with the abacus altogether, relying
apparently on a visual image. Using methods derived from the study of

working memory, two Japanese psychologists, Hatano and Osawa (1983), showed that use of the sketchpad lay at the root of this skill, with the result that it could be disrupted by concurrent visuo-spatial, but not verbal activity.

In contrast, concurrent verbal activity can substantially interfere with the operation of the Articulatory Loop which appears to comprise a system involving two components, a temporary auditory store, and a speech-based rehearsal process. It is possible to get some information about each of these in turn by trying the following short tests. In each case, read the sequence of words, then look away and attempt to repeat them back; then check whether you were able to do this accurately and in the appropriate order. I shall include sequences of both five items and six items in each case:

PEN DAY RIG COW HOT
RIG DAY PEN SUP HOT COW

Now try the next two:

MAP CAN MAX MAD CAP
MAX CAP MAD MAP MAT CAN

Most people find the *MAD MAX* set of words considerably harder than the others. The reason for this is that the memory store involved in temporarily holding strings of unrelated words is based on the phonological or sound characteristics of those words. Words that are similar in sound tend to be confused within this store, leading to poorer performance. Now try the next set:

HARM WIT BOND TWICE YIELD
SOME YIELD BOND TWICE HARM WIT

Now attempt the next set:

ORGANIZATION INDIVIDUAL UNIVERSITY CONSIDERABLE ASSOCIATION

UNIVERSITY INDIVIDUAL ASSOCIATION OPPORTUNITY ORGANIZATION CONSIDERABLE

In this case, people usually find the short words considerably easier than the long ones. The reason here is that we maintain words in our temporary memory store by rehearsing them, subvocally saying them to ourselves. The system of rehearsal operates in real time, and consequently long words are rehearsed more slowly than short, allowing more fading of the memory trace between successive rehearsals.

If you were to stop yourself rehearsing by subvocally repeating some irrelevant words such as "the" while reading and recalling the words, then you would find that your memory performance dropped substantially, but that you avoided both the similarity and the word-length effects. The reason for this is that you need subvocal rehearsal to feed the printed words into your auditory-verbal store. If the subvocal rehearsal system is kept fully occupied repeating the word "the", then the written material does not enter the store, and neither word-length nor similarity effects are found. Instead you rely on some alternative memory in terms of the visual or semantic characteristics of the words, systems that are rather less efficient than the phonological store for briefly retaining this type of material.

By using experiments of this kind we have been able to find out a good deal about the Articulatory Loop system. But what function does the system serve? This problem was made particularly acute by the discovery of patients who have a specific deficit of short-term phonological storage (Shallice & Warrington, 1970; Vallar & Baddeley, 1982). Such patients appear to cope with life remarkably well, raising the dreadful thought that this system may be very useful for keeping experimental psychologists happy but of not much general significance. It might, as my colleague Jim Reason rather unkindly suggested, turn out to be "nothing but a pimple on the face of cognition".

In our research we have been particularly concerned with this question and in particular have been interested in the cognitive abilities of the rare patients who are found to have a very specific deficit in this system. Close investigation shows that such patients do have problems in comprehending certain types of sentences, particularly those in which comprehension requires the listener to hold the surface characteristics of initial words across several intervening words. One example of such material is provided by self-embedded sentences such as "The soldier whom the man had met on the train earlier in the week was wearing a large hat". Such patients have difficulty in working out who was wearing the hat in these circumstances.

A much more dramatic impairment was, however, revealed in a study of such a patient in which she was required to learn phonologically novel items, such as would be the case if you were learning the vocabulary of a foreign language. Our patient proved quite incapable of learning even a single new vocabulary item when these were presented auditorily, although when she was allowed to read the foreign words, she did show some learning, but her learning was by no means as good as that of control subjects matched for age and background. On the other hand, when required to learn to associate pairs of familiar and meaningful words, her learning capacity proved to be quite normal (Baddeley, Papagno, & Vallar, 1988).

It appears then that the short-term phonological memory system is necessary for the long-term learning of novel verbal material. As such, it should play an important role in a child's learning the vocabulary of his or her native language. A colleague, Susan Gathercole, and I explored this question using a sample of children who started school in Cambridge at the age of 4–5 years. We tested the short-term phonological memory of our children by requiring them to echo back spoken unfamiliar nonwords varying in length and complexity. We also tested their vocabulary, speaking a word and requiring them

6

to point to a picture of the item denoted, and in addition measured their non-verbal intelligence and any reading skills they might have acquired. A year later we re-tested them using the same tasks.

When we analysed our results we found a close relationship between performance on the phonological memory task involving non-word repetition and vocabulary score. The relationship was still there when we allowed for other factors such as non-verbal intelligence and slight differences in age. One year later the relationship still held. Furthermore, the increase in vocabulary over the intervening year was predicted by their initial non-word repetition skills (Gathercole & Baddeley, 1988). Our results suggest, therefore, that the short-term phonological store plays a crucial role in the long-term acquisition of language. So if the Articulatory Loop is a pimple on the face of cognition, then it is a rather important pimple!

Long-term memory

We have so far concentrated almost exclusively on one aspect of working memory, the Articulatory Loop subsystem. Space availability forbids the provision of similar detail about the rest of working memory; the interested reader is referred to Baddeley (1986). Meanwhile, we must move on to discuss long-term memory. Once again, it seems unlikely that this reflects a single unitary system, although there is still considerable disagreement as to how long-term memory should be fractionated. We shall begin by discussing two theoretical distinctions that have proved influential in recent years, namely that between *semantic* and *episodic* memory, and that between *procedural* and *declarative* learning. We shall then go on to talk about two aspects of memory that are defined in terms of their real-world manifestations rather than their theoretical underpinning, namely *prospective* memory and *autobiographical* memory. This will be followed by an analysis of the points at which human memory is particularly vulnerable to bias and distortion.

In the early 1970s the Canadian psychologist Endel Tulving emphasized a distinction between two aspects of memory that, as he points out, had long been implicit in the culture, but had not been explicitly acknowledged by experimental psychologists. He drew a distinction between episodic memory, by which he meant the conscious recollection of personally experienced events, and semantic memory or knowledge of the world (Tulving, 1972). An example of an episodic memory would be my recall of the experience of having breakfast this morning, or of meeting someone a year ago on holiday. Semantic memory, on the other hand, involves such factual knowledge as how many inches there are in a foot, what the capital of France is, or the fact that people often have cornflakes for breakfast.

There is no doubt that, as Tulving points out, there are very many differences between, for example, my memory of watching a rugby game on television yesterday afternoon and my knowing that a rugby team constitutes

7

15 players. What is, however, much less clear is whether these two examples reflect the operation of quite separate systems within the brain, as Tulving initially suggested, or whether they reflect the same system operating under very different conditions. This latter view might, for example, suggest that semantic memory represents the accumulation of information from many, many episodes or layers of experience, implying that rather than being a separate system, semantic memory is made up from multiple episodic memories.

A distinction that appears to have much stronger experimental support is that between procedural and declarative learning. Procedural learning comprises the acquisition of skills, such as learning to type, whereby demonstration of learning is reflected in the more efficient performance of the skill. In this respect it is different from declarative learning, such as remembering going to a typing class, which is essentially the acquisition of new knowledge or experience. Procedural learning is knowing *how*; declarative learning is knowing *that*.

The most powerful evidence for such a distinction comes from studies of amnesic patients who have a major long-term memory deficit following brain damage. This can be produced by a number of causes including chronic alcoholism, brain damage due to head injury, stroke, or through a viral infection, as was the case with Clive Wearing described earlier. Amnesic patients typically have great difficulty in recalling what they had for breakfast, where they are, or in remembering their way around the house or ward. Typically they would have normal language and normal working memory, and might have a relatively good memory for events occurring well before the onset of their illness or accident. They would, however, show very poor performance on most standard tests of the memory laboratory such as learning lists of words, recalling complex patterns, or recognizing previously presented faces or pictures.

However, despite the general and often profound memory deficit shown, such patients typically show quite normal learning on a remarkably wide range of other tasks. These range from classical conditioning, in which the patient learns to associate a sound with a puff of air and to close his or her eyes in anticipation, through motor skills such as learning to type or for a pianist learning a new tune, to perceptual skills. These might, for example, involve learning to read mirror-writing, or to find anomalies in complex pictures, where performance speeds up with practice, just as it does in people with normal memory. Similarly, a range of puzzles and problem tasks can be acquired at a normal rate, including jigsaw puzzles, and even the solving of complex problems such as the Tower of Hanoi task (Parkin, 1987).

Although such amnesic patients show very poor learning of words, there are certain conditions under which their verbal learning also proves to be normal. One of the most striking of these is one in which the subject is given a series of words to learn, and is then cued to remember them by being presented with a fragment of the original. For example one of the words might be PERFUME. If tested by recognition, with the patient required to say which of a number of words had been presented before, then amnesic patients perform very poorly. However, given the letters P**F*M* and asked to come up with the first word that fits the letter pattern, then the amnesic patient will perform extremely well, showing virtually as much advantage from previously having seen the target word as a normal subject asked to perform in this way.

What all these examples have in common is that they allow the patient to demonstrate learning, without the need for conscious awareness of the learning process. Typically, indeed, amnesic patients will deny having encountered the task before, at the same time as they are showing clear evidence of learning. This therefore seems to argue for two separate aspects of memory, one involving the capacity to reflect on prior experience, a capacity that is grossly impaired in amnesic patients. The second involves the apparently automatic display of learning in tasks where recollection of the learning event is unnecessary; such procedural learning appears to be intact in densely amnesic patients.

Long-term memory therefore appears to involve two separate types of learning: declarative and procedural. Declarative learning appears to be associated with conscious recollection of the past, and its adequate functioning appears to be disrupted by damage to a number of cortical and subcortical structures including the temporal lobes, the hippocampi, and the mamillary bodies. In contrast, damage to these areas does not appear to prevent the more automatic process of procedural learning. Whether procedural learning will ultimately prove to be a single unitary system, or whether procedural tasks merely have in common the fact that they do not require conscious recollection, is still a very open question.

The psychology of memory succeeded in separating itself from the more speculative philosophical approach to memory by dint of simplification. In particular, the father of research on human memory, the nineteenth-century German psychologist Hermann Ebbinghaus, was the first person to demonstrate the possibility of quantitative exploration of the characteristics of human memory. He did so by reducing the complexities of real-world memory to the simple learning by rote of meaningless verbal material, teaching himself to recite long sequences of invented non-words such as TOV, ZIL, and KIJ, and carefully measuring those factors that influenced rate of learning and forgetting (Ebbinghaus, 1913).

REAL-WORLD IMPLICATIONS

The Ebbinghaus tradition played an important role in the development of the psychology of memory, but it has the weakness that it tends to concentrate too heavily on simplified and apparently soluble problems, and to neglect the

9

richness of memory in the world at large. There have been increasing efforts to link the memory laboratory and the world, typically by taking laboratory phenomena and looking for their real-world implications, as for example in the case of our studies on the role of the Articulatory Loop system of working memory. Equally important, however, is a willingness to take aspects of memory that are important in everyday life, and ask what are the implications of these for current theories of memory. I shall briefly describe two such areas, one concerned with *prospective memory*, or remembering to do things, while the other, *autobiographical memory*, refers to our capacity to remember the events of our own lives.

Prospective memory

If people tell you that they have a terrible memory, it typically implies that they are prone to making memory lapses such as forgetting appointments or failing to remember where they have left things around the house. How is this type of memory related to the system studied by psychologists in the laboratory? Arnold Wilkins and I became interested in the problem of studying this in the mid-1970s (Wilkins & Baddeley, 1978). We wanted to simulate the task of remembering to take pills four times a day, and in order to do so Arnold invented a simple but ingenious device. This comprised a light-tight box containing a digital watch and a film. When a button on the box was pressed, the dial of the watch was illuminated and the time registered on the film, which was then moved on. The subjects were instructed to press the button at four specified times each day for a period of a week. We carefully selected two groups of subjects, one that we knew to be very good at remembering lists of words, and one that was rather poor at this task. We were interested in whether the two groups would differ in remembering to "take their pills".

We found that significant differences between the two groups did indeed occur, but that the subjects who were particularly good at remembering words were the least punctual and accurate in pressing the button, a phenomenon we subsequently labelled "the absent-minded professor effect". It seems likely that remembering to do things at the right time depends on things other than having a good general memory. There is, for example, evidence that elderly people become significantly poorer at learning new material, but report fewer memory lapses. While some of this apparent improvement with age may simply be due to the fact that elderly people are more likely to forget their memory lapses before they are asked to report them, other evidence suggests that this is not the only cause. In one study, for example, where subjects were instructed to telephone the experimenter at a specified time in the future, elderly people were consistently more reliable and accurate than the young (Moscovitch, 1982). The reason for this is probably that they have learned to organize their lives in a much more structured way than the young, hence compensating for a memory system that is perhaps not quite what it used to be.

Does remembering to do things therefore depend on an entirely different system from the rest of memory? We now know that this is not the case. In order to obtain a good and reliable estimate of everyday memory problems, Barbara Wilson, who at that time was working at Rivermead Rehabilitation Centre in Oxford, came up with a novel kind of memory test. This involved requiring the patient to perform a number of tasks, each of which attempted to test objectively a situation in which patients report a tendency to memory lapses. For example, they would be required to learn the name of a person in a photograph, to learn a new route, to memorize and subsequently recognize photographs of new people, and to indicate orientation in time and place. In addition, a number of tests of prospective memory were included; for example the patient was asked for some small personal item such as a comb, and this was secreted in a drawer, with the instruction that the patient should remember to ask for it at the end of the test (Wilson, Cockburn, & Baddeley, 1985).

The Rivermead Behavioural Memory Test was subsequently validated using a large number of patients attending the Rehabilitation Centre. It proved to be a good measure of everyday memory, correlating quite highly ($r = .75$) with the observation of memory lapses in the patients made by therapists over many hours of treatment. It also proved to be the case that prospective memory was impaired in those patients who performed poorly on other tests of memory, including such traditional tasks as learning lists of words and recalling complex figures (Wilson, Baddeley, & Cockburn, 1988). Indeed, a subsequent study which applied the test to normal elderly people showed that those items that tested prospective memory were particularly susceptible to the effects of age (Cockburn & Smith, 1988).

In conclusion then, it appears that remembering to do things does depend on the same system as is reflected in standard laboratory memory tasks. In addition, however, it probably depends rather crucially on both the way in which one organizes one's life, and on how important it is to remember that particular feature. Forgetting an appointment, birthday, or anniversary can be hurtful in a way that forgetting an address or telephone number is not; the reason is that forgetting to do things certainly in part reflects the fallibility of our memory, but it also reflects the importance that we place on the event in question.

Autobiographical memory

People often claim of elderly relatives that they have a marvellous memory. When questioned further, this usually means not that they make no errors of prospective memory, but rather that they appear to show an amazing capacity to recollect the events from their earlier life, sometimes prompting

11

the speculation that age somehow enhances early memories. On the whole the evidence does not support this view; elderly people tend to be poorer at recalling both recent and distant events. They are, however, likely to spend rather more time reminiscing about the past, and hence to revive and go over certain old memories in a way that makes them perhaps more accessible than they were during the middle years when attention was focused more firmly on the present and the future.

The capacity to recollect events from one's earlier life is termed *auto-biographical memory*. The systematic study of this aspect of memory began in the 1880s with the work of Sir Francis Galton (1883), but was then neglected until a relatively recent revival of interest. The reason for its neglect is probably the complexity of the topic, with the difficulty of turning rich but potentially unreliable information into readily quantifiable and verifiable results.

In my own case, the development of interest in autobiographical memory stemmed from a discovery that amnesic patients, who were otherwise very similar, might differ quite markedly in their capacity to recollect their own earlier life. In order to explore this further, we adopted the technique originally pioneered by Galton, whereby the patient is given a word such as *river*, and asked to try to recollect some specific personally experienced event that is associated with a river. The resulting memory is then classified as to its richness, specificity, and reliability.

Using these criteria, we found that patients tended to fall into one of three categories. Some patients appeared to have relatively normal memories of the period before their illness, whereas others appeared to view their past as if through a dense cloud. Yet a third group proved to be particularly intriguing since they gave what appeared to be rich and detailed recollections which subsequently proved to be quite fictitious. Such confabulating patients were typically those with severe damage to the frontal lobes, coupled with an amnesic deficit. The frontal lobes appear to be responsible among other things for the control of behaviour, for the operation of the central executive component of working memory, for example, and a deficit in this system appears to lead to confabulation. Such confabulation is worth discussing in rather more detail since it has interesting implications for the veracity of autobiographical memory in normal subjects, raising as it does the question of how we separate truth, or approximate truth, from fantasy in recalling our own past.

The confabulated memory sometimes has an amusing and almost sur-realistic character, as in the following recollection produced by a patient, NW, who in response to the cue word *make* described making a gramophone turntable at school. On being re-tested on a later occasion he did not report this, and I attempted to prompt him by mentioning that he had described something made at school, whereupon he produced the following:

ADB: Can you think of anything you made at school that is striking?
NW: An Australian wombat.
ADB: An Australian wombat?
NW: Ashtray, something different.
ADB: That does sound different. How do you make an Australian wombat ashtray?
NW: Get a piece of wood, let your imagination go...
ADB: Did you make anything else that you can think of, a bit more conventional?
NW: No I don't think so; I made a daffodil, again in wood. That was all to do with the school play.
ADB: How was it to do with the school play?
NW: There was a bowl of fruit and flowers which had to be given to the queen, Queen Diadem. All the various people had to make a flower. We were told to make something out of wood; I happened to be asked to make the daffodil, one of the easier pieces.

As this particular recollection might suggest, one occasionally wonders whether the patient is not simply teasing the experimenter. I think not, for a number of reasons. First of all, such confabulations are by no means limited to discussions with psychologists. In the case of one of our patients RJ, for example, his wife reported that when he was home one weekend he turned to her in bed and asked

"Why do you keep telling people we are married?"
"But we are married, we've got three children", his wife responded.
"That doesn't necessarily mean we're married".

Whereupon his wife got out of bed and produced the wedding photographs, to which her husband commented, "Well that chap does look like me, but it's not!"

The same patient also would hold with considerable stubbornness to his often misguided memory, insisting for example that he should be in occupational therapy next and not physiotherapy, or that his luggage had been stored in a loft, and climbing on a toilet seat in order to access the non-existent loft. As the last incident implies, he was certainly willing to act on his confabulations, and on one occasion was found wheeling a fellow patient down the road. When stopped he reported that he was taking him to show his friend the sewage works that he was working on. He had indeed been involved in building a sewage works as a civil engineer, but that was many years ago and many miles away.

So why does confabulation occur? We suspect that it requires a combination of two things, first of all an impaired or clouded autobiographical memory, and second, a deficit in that aspect of the central executive of working memory that is necessary for controlling and evaluating behaviour. We believe that given the difficult task of retrieving a specific memory associated with a highly constrained cue word, patients with a deficit in the

13

central executive are unable to access a genuine memory. What they produce instead is some form of association which they accept and elaborate. Without the adequate control of the process of retrieval, what is produced is something rather closer to a free association or a dream.

Normal subjects do not on the whole confabulate, partly because they have better access to their memory trace, and so have less need to invent memories, and partly because they have a much better checking mechanism for the plausibility of whatever their memory might produce. I suspect, however, that this is a matter of degree rather than an absolute difference. On the whole we do not go in for florid confabulation, but in subtler ways our memories can be highly unreliable, and I would like to conclude by reviewing some of the ways in which our memories are fallible.

FALLIBILITY

Memories are systems for storing information, and as such are required to do three things: to take in the necessary information, to store it, and to retrieve it at the appropriate time. Human memory is potentially fallible at each of these points.

Consider first the way in which information is registered in memory. This of course depends on attention. If we do not attend to something, then we are very unlikely to remember it, despite the claims to the contrary of those who try to sell courses of sleep learning and other allegedly painless roads to knowledge. What we attend to is determined by our interests and prejudices, as was demonstrated many years ago by the Princeton social psychologists Hastorf and Cantril (1954). They described a football game between Dartmouth and Princeton that aroused passionate commitment on both sides. Princeton had a particularly talented quarterback who was injured early in the game, a game that subsequently became increasingly violent. Hastorf and Cantril report the account of the game given in the Princeton and Dartmouth college newspapers.

> This observer has never seen quite such a disgusting exhibit of so-called "sport". Both teams were guilty but the blame must be laid primarily on Dartmouth's doorstep. Princeton, obviously the better team, had no reason to rough up Dartmouth. Looking at the situation rationally, we don't see why the [Dartmouth] Indians should make a deliberate attempt to cripple Dick Kazmaier or any other Princeton player. The Dartmouth psychology, however, is not rational itself.

> However, the Dartmouth-Princeton game set the stage for the other type of dirty football. A type which may be termed as an unjustifiable accusation. Dick Kazmaier was injured early in the game . . . after this incident [the coach] instilled the old see-what-they-did-go-get-them attitude into his players. His talk got results. Gene Howard and Jim Millar [from Dartmouth] were both injured. Both had dropped back to pass, had passed, and were standing unprotected in the back field. Result: one bad leg and one leg broken. The game was rough and did get a bit out

14

of hand in the third quarter. Yet most of the roughing penalties were called against Princeton.

It is not hard to guess which newspaper is which.

But is this a memory effect? Hastorf and Cantril investigated this by showing a film of the game to both Dartmouth and Princeton students, asking them to note when they observed a piece of foul play. In the case of Dartmouth infringements there was a clear difference between the two with Princeton students reporting a mean of 9.8 while the Dartmouth students reported 4.3.

The tendency to see and remember things from an egocentric viewpoint is of course not limited to situations involving conflict. A particularly intriguing example of rather more subtle effects of bias was shown in Neisser's (1981) analysis of the testimony given by John Dean in the Watergate investigation. You may recall that the press were so struck by Dean's apparent capacity to remember specific conversations in great detail that they dubbed him the man with the tape recorder memory. When the actual tape recordings of the conversations subsequently became available it proved possible to check the accuracy of this claim.

In terms of the gist of the conversations, Dean's recollection was in fact reasonably accurate, but the detail showed considerable distortion. The nature of the distortion was interesting in that it typically resulted in Dean's own role being perceived as more important and more central, an egocentric bias that I suspect most of us would show in a similar situation.

To return to our students watching the football game, bias in their viewpoint was clearly one factor, but another could well have been the degree of emotion generated by the "big game". What role does emotion play in memory? This is a point of some importance in the case of a witness recalling a violent crime.

I was telephoned one Sunday evening by someone who introduced himself as a detective from the San Diego Police Force. He was involved in the investigation of a multiple murderer who had the unsavoury habit of slashing his victims' throats. Having killed six people, the seventh survived and identified someone as the attacker. What, I was asked, would be the influence of extreme emotion on the victim's memory?

The answer is that on the whole introducing emotion tends to reduce the accuracy with which an eyewitness can remember a crime; it does not apparently imprint the incident indelibly on the memory, as one might guess. However, when asked if the level of emotion generated in the experimental studies was equivalent to the level that the San Diego slasher's victim was likely to have experienced, I had to admit that it was certainly not. Even the most dedicated experimental psychologists do not, I am happy to say, threaten to cut their subjects' throats, even in the interests of science.

It is clear then that bias and emotion can both cause distortion in what gets into memory. Suppose, however, that information does get into memory, what factors will influence the durability of memory storage? While information on speed of forgetting is still surprisingly sparse, the evidence on the whole suggests that differential rates of forgetting for different kinds of material is not very common. Needless to say, increased forgetting can be produced by brain damage, or by the more temporary effects of a blow on the head. The ability to remember an incident can, however, also be substantially impaired by presenting further interfering or misleading information.

This again has obvious practical implications in the case of eyewitness testimony, and there has been a great deal of interest in the distortions of memory that can be produced when leading questions are inserted into the subsequent interrogation of the witness. Choice of words can for example bias the subject's subsequent recall. In one study, Loftus and Palmer (1974) showed subjects a film of a car crash, and subsequently questioned them about various details. One question concerned the speed at which one car was moving when it hit the other. Some subjects were asked "About how fast were the cars going when they hit each other?", while for others the word "hit" was replaced with "contacted", "bumped", "collided", or "smashed". Estimated speeds ranged from 31.8 miles per hour for "contacted" to 40.8 for "smashed". When questioned a week later as to whether any glass had been broken, subjects who had encountered the word "smashed" were significantly more likely to report, falsely, that glass had been broken.

In other studies, Loftus and her collaborators were able to change subjects' views on a whole range of features of observed incidents, including the colour of cars, whether a stop sign or a yield (give way) sign was present, while in another study many subjects were induced to report the occurrence of a non-existent barn. In all these cases, the distorted information was introduced parenthetically during an earlier question, and only subsequently probed directly. Subjects do not appear to be aware of the source of their mistake, and allowing them a second guess, or paying them a substantial amount for making the correct response had no effect on the bias.

At this point, Loftus and Palmer began to conclude that a permanent modification had been made in the underlying memory trace, with the old information destroyed by the new. However, as they fully realized, failure to find the old trace did not necessarily mean that it had been destroyed, rather than simply made unavailable.

Indeed a subsequent study by Bekerian and Bowers (1983) showed that the old trace had survived, and given an appropriate method of retrieval, it could be accessed. The studies by Loftus typically involved questioning the subject about the incident in a relatively unstructured way. Bekerian and Bowers showed that if the questions followed the order of the events in strict sequence, then subjects were able to access the original information, and to escape from the bias introduced by subsequent questions. In short, the

16

Loftus effect is not due to destruction of the memory trace but is due to interfering with its retrieval.

RETRIEVAL

Before discussing further potential distortions in human memory that occur at the retrieval stage, it is perhaps worth describing the process of retrieval in somewhat more detail. One way of doing so is to draw an analogy between human memory and an inanimate storage system such as a library. A library could operate merely as a passive storehouse in which books were piled up as they arrived. Such a system would, however, not be very easy to use unless one virtually always needed one of the last few books to have entered the system. If one needed to access books on the basis of subject, then it is of course essential to have a subject catalogue, and if a book has not been correctly catalogued when it came in, then retrieving it is going to be a very difficult and haphazard process. The secret of a good memory, as of a good library, is that of organization; good learning typically goes with the systematic encoding of incoming material, integrating and relating it to what is already known.

Suppose, however, that one has encoded the material appropriately, what is the process whereby one calls up the right memory at the right time? While we are still some way from fully understanding the retrieval process, one feature is captured by what Tulving has termed *encoding specificity*. On the whole, we access a piece of information by feeding in a fragment of what we wish to recall; the more accurate and complete the fragment, the better the chance of retrieval.

One aspect of this that has been known for centuries is the phenomenon of *context dependency*, the tendency for what is learned in one situation to be best recalled in that situation. The philosopher John Locke recounts the tale of a young man who learned to dance. His lessons always occurred in an attic that had a large trunk. Locke reports that while the young man could dance extremely well in the attic, if the trunk was removed he was no longer able to remember the steps.

How good is the scientific evidence for such context dependency? While there are not too many experiments on memory for dancing, there certainly is evidence that memory may be influenced by context. For example, Duncan Godden and I studied memory in deep-sea divers. We had our divers learn lists of words either on the beach, or 10 feet under the sea, and subsequently recall them in the wet or the dry environment. What we found was that regardless of where they learned the words, they remembered about 40 per cent fewer when they were trying to recall them in the opposite environment (Godden & Baddeley, 1975).

Such a result could have rather dramatic implications; would all our students show dramatically good memory if their examinations were held in the lecture theatre, and will they forget everything once they have left the university? While the latter suggestion may indeed be true, it is probably not a result of context dependency: effects as large as those we obtained occur only with a very dramatic change in environment. Less marked changes can produce detectable effects, but on the whole studies that look at examination performance in the original lecture room versus the novel examination hall do not suggest any major difference in performance.

The comparatively small effect of environmental context under normal conditions probably reflects the fact that when we are learning, the surroundings are probably not a particularly salient feature of the situation. The internal environment, however, can have subtle but powerful effects. Mood, for instance, can have a contextual effect on memory, with subjects in a sad mood typically being much more likely to recollect earlier unhappy events from their life than subjects in a happy mood, and vice versa (Bower, 1981). This can have a powerful effect on depression since it will of course tend to make the sad person even sadder, which in turn will cause him or her to remember even more depressing events, locking the unfortunate person into a vicious spiral of increasingly depressive rumination. This is in fact thought to be an important factor in the maintenance of depression, and some developments in the cognitive treatment of depression are principally concerned to reverse this process.

Other changes in internal states can of course be induced by drugs, producing so-called *state dependency* effects. Such effects can, for example, be produced by alcohol: what is learned drunk is best recalled drunk. Sometimes alcoholics will hide money and drink while in a drunken state, and then forget where it has been located, only to remember once they are drunk again. Such drug-based state dependency played an important role in what is claimed to be the first detective story written, *The Moonstone* by Wilkie Collins (published 1868).

Retrieval then is probably one of the most vulnerable points in human memory, with biased situations leading to failure to recall, or possibly partial recall which in turn is subject to distortion when we try to interpret our incomplete memory. A very nice example of such distortion is given by the Swiss psychologist Jean Piaget, who reports having had a very clear and detailed memory of an incident when he was a baby, whereby an attempt was made to kidnap him and was thwarted by his nursemaid. He reports having a vivid memory of the incident, full of detail. The nursemaid was rewarded for her valour by being given a watch. Many years later she returned the watch to the family saying that she had recently had a religious conversion and wished to confess an earlier sin. It appears that the incident had simply not occurred, but had been invented by her in the hopes of currying favour with her employers. Piaget's vivid "memory", it appears, was constructed from the many accounts he had heard of the incident as he grew up (Loftus, 1979, pp. 62–63).

PSYCHOANALYTIC THEORY

Before concluding, I should say something about one approach to forgetting that has had considerable influence on twentieth-century western culture, namely the psychoanalytic view of forgetting as the result of repression. Freud suggests that much forgetting occurs because the events concerned are associated with unpleasant events that evoke anxiety, and call up an automatic process that bars them from conscious awareness. In his *Psychopathology of Everyday Life*, Freud (1938) reports many incidents which he attributes to repression. I am afraid, however, that attempts to demonstrate repression under more controlled conditions have not proved particularly encouraging (see Baddeley, 1990, chap. 15). There certainly is a general tendency for people recalling their earlier life to remember the pleasant events rather than the unpleasant, at least when they are in a reasonably happy state of mind. Whether this represents active repression, however, is open to question; it is quite possible that this simply reflects a tendency to choose to reflect on and tell others about our successes rather than our failures, leading to pleasant events being rehearsed more. Certainly, attempts to demonstrate the influence of repression under more rigidly controlled conditions tend to suggest that it is not a major feature in the vast amount of forgetting that most people exhibit, although in the rare cases of hysterical amnesia, something much more closely approaching the Freudian explanation probably does apply.

To conclude then, there is no doubt that human memory is eminently fallible. However, its sources of fallibility are often reflections of its strengths. Bias in feeding information into the memory system certainly does occur. However, bias is simply the consequence of selection; if we did not select what was interesting and important, then our memory systems would become overloaded with trivial and irrelevant information.

There is no doubt that forgetting occurs on a massive scale, something that characterizes memory systems in humans but not in computers or libraries. However, such forgetting is on the whole benign. Typically we remember what is salient and important to us, and forget the trivial and irrelevant detail. It is only when such detail subsequently becomes crucial, as in the testimony of an eyewitness, that the fallibility of our memory becomes particularly obvious. In other situations, if we need to remember something in enormous detail, then we write it down.

Finally, retrieval presents a clear bottleneck in our capacity to access what we have previously learned. Even here, however, the context dependency effect means that we are more likely to remember the information that is relevant to the situation we are in, in preference to information that is relevant to some other distant setting, surely a sensible adaptation of a limited retrieval system. In conclusion, I should like to suggest that although eminently fallible, human memory is an elegant system; nobody should be without one.

ACKNOWLEDGEMENT

This chapter is based on my contribution to Thomas Butler's (1989) *Memory: History, Culture and the Mind* published by Basil Blackwell of Oxford. I am grateful to the publisher for permission to reproduce it.

FURTHER READING

Baddeley A. D. (1993). *Your memory: A user's guide*, 2nd edn. Harmondsworth: Penguin.
Baddeley, A. D. (1990). *Human memory: Theory and practice*. Hove: Lawrence Erlbaum.
Cohen, G. (1989). *Memory in the real world*. Hove: Lawrence Erlbaum.
Parkin, A. J. (1987). *Memory and amnesia: An introduction*. Oxford: Basil Blackwell.

REFERENCES

Atkinson, R. C., & Shiffrin, R. M. (1971). The control of short-term memory. *Scientific American*, *225*, 82–90.
Baddeley, A. D. (1982). *Your memory: A user's guide*. Harmondsworth: Penguin.
Baddeley, A. D. (1986). *Working memory*. Oxford: Oxford University Press.
Baddeley, A. D. (1990). *Human memory: Theory and practice*. Hove: Lawrence Erlbaum.
Baddeley, A. D., Papagno, C., & Vallar, G. (1988). When long-term learning depends on short-term storage. *Journal of Memory and Language*, *27*, 586–595.
Bekerian, D. A., & Bowers, J. M. (1983). Eyewitness testimony: Were we misled? *Journal of Experimental Psychology: Human Learning and Memory*, *9*, 139–145.
Bower, G. H. (1981). Mood and memory. *American Psychologist*, *36*, 129–148.
Cockburn, J., & Smith, P. T. (1988). Effects of age and intelligence on everyday memory tasks. In M. M. Gruneberg, P. Morris, & R. N. Sykes (Eds) *Practical aspects of memory: Current research and issues. Clinical and educational implications* (vol. 2, pp. 132–136). Chichester: Wiley.
Ebbinghaus, H. (1913). *Memory* (H. Ruyer & C. E. Bussenius, trans.) New York: Teachers College, Columbia University (original work published 1985).
Freud, S. (1938). Psychopathology of everyday life. In A. A. Brill (Ed.) *The writings of Sigmund Freud*. New York: Modern Library.
Galton, F. (1883). *Inquiries in human faculty and its development*. London: Dent.
Gathercole, S. E., & Baddeley, A. D. (1988). Development of vocabulary in children and short-term phonological memory. *Journal of Memory and Language*, *28*, 200–213.
Godden, D., & Baddeley, A. D. (1975). Context-dependent memory in two natural environments: On land and under water. *British Journal of Psychology*, *66*, 325–331.
Hastorf, A. A., & Cantril, H. (1954). They saw a game: A case study. *Journal of Abnormal and Social Psychology*, *97*, 399–401.

Hatano, G., & Osawa, K. (1983). Digit memory of grant experts in abacus-derived mental calculation. *Cognition*, *15*, 95–110.

Loftus, E. F. (1979). *Eyewitness testimony*. Cambridge, MA: Harvard University Press.

Loftus, E. F., & Palmer, J. C. (1974). Reconstruction of automobile destruction: An example of the interaction between language and memory. *Journal of Verbal Learning and Verbal Behavior*, *13*, 585–589.

Miller, J. (1986). Interview with Clive Wearing. *Prisoner of Consciousness*. Broadcast in the UK by Channel 4 in the Equinox Series, September.

Moscovitch, M. (1982). A neuropsychological approach to memory and perception. In F. I. M. Craik & S. Trehub (Eds) *Aging and cognitive processes* (pp. 55–78). New York: Plenum.

Neisser, U. (1981). John Dean's memory: A case study. *Cognition*, *9*, 1–22.

Parkin, A. J. (1987). *Memory and amnesia: An introduction*. Oxford: Basil Blackwell.

Shallice, T., & Warrington, E. K. (1970). Independent functioning of verbal memory stores: A neuropsychological study. *Quarterly Journal of Experimental Psychology*, *22*, 261–273.

Tulving, E. (1972). Episodic and semantic memory. In E. Tulving & W. Donaldson (Eds) *Organization of memory* (pp. 381–403). New York: Academic Press.

Vallar, G., & Baddeley, A. D. (1982). Short-term forgetting and the articulatory loop. *Quarterly Journal of Experimental Psychology*, *34A*, 53–60.

Wilkins, A. J., & Baddeley, A. D. (1978). Remembering to recall in everyday life: An approach to absentmindedness. In M. M. Gruneberg, P. E. Morris, & R. N. Sykes (Eds) *Practical aspects of memory* (pp. 27–34). London: Academic Press.

Wilson, B., Baddeley, A. D., & Cockburn, J. (1988). Trials, tribulations and triumphs in the development of a test of everyday memory. In M. M. Gruneberg, P. Morris, & R. N. Sykes (Eds) *Practical aspects of memory: Current research and issues. Memory in everyday life* (vol. 1, pp. 249–254). Chichester: Wiley.

Wilson, B., Cockburn, J., & Baddeley, A. D. (1985). *The Rivermead behavioural memory test*. Bury St Edmunds: Thames Valley Test Company.

2

ATTENTION

Michael W. Eysenck

Royal Holloway, University of London, Surrey, England

The term "attention" has been used in a number of different ways. It is sometimes used to mean concentration, as in the expression "Pay attention!" A related use of the term is as a process that varies as a function of an individual's level of arousal: someone who is aroused is attentive to his or her environment, whereas someone who is low in arousal or drowsy is not. However, the most common usage of attention is in connection with selectivity of processing. This usage was emphasized by the nineteenth-century psychologist William James (1890):

> Everyone knows what attention is. It is the taking possession of the mind, in clear and vivid form, of one out of what seem several simultaneously possible objects or trains of thought. Focalisation, concentration, of consciousness are of its essence. It implies withdrawal from some things in order to deal effectively with others. (pp. 403–404)

In order to investigate how efficiently we are able to attend selectively, researchers have conducted much research on focused attention. In such research, subjects are presented with two or more sets of stimuli at the same time. They are instructed to process one set of stimuli while ignoring the other set or sets. The amount of processing of the to-be-ignored stimuli which occurs provides an indication of how successfully attention can be focused on the stimuli that the experimenter has identified as important.

Another issue which is important in attention research concerns the number of things that can be attended to at the same time. Once again, William James (1890) had an important contribution to make:

> The number of things we may attend to is altogether indefinite, depending on the power of the individual intellect, on the form of the apprehension, and on what things are. ... But however numerous the things, they can only be known in a single pulse of consciousness for which they form one complex "object". (p. 405)

In order to investigate the extent to which more than one thing can be attended to at once, it has been customary to carry out studies on divided attention. In essence, subjects are generally presented two stimulus inputs or tasks at the same time. They are instructed to do their best to perform both of the tasks, and their success or otherwise in doing this provides an indication of the capacity of the attentional system.

While the distinction between focused and divided attention is of fundamental importance, there are other distinctions worth noting. First, attention can be directed towards either the external environment or to the internal environment, which consists of our own thoughts. In practice, most of the research on attention has concerned the external environment rather than the internal environment, presumably because researchers can control those aspects of the external environment which receive attention much more readily than they can the internal environment. Second, it is important to distinguish between attentional processes in the various sense modalities. For example, it may be easier to focus attention on a single stimulus input in some modalities than others, and so we really need to consider the various modalities separately. However, only the visual and auditory modalities have been investigated with any thoroughness, and so our coverage will concentrate on those modalities.

FOCUSED AUDITORY ATTENTION

One of the key issues with respect to focused auditory attention is whether it is possible to attend to one auditory message while successfully ignoring other auditory messages that are presented at the same time. This issue was first examined systematically by Cherry (1953), who devised the dichotic listening task. Subjects performing this task listen through headphones which deliver one message to the left ear and a different message to the right ear. They are instructed to repeat back (or shadow) the message presented to one ear while ignoring the message presented to the other ear. Cherry found that the subjects found it reasonably straightforward to follow the instructions even when the two messages were spoken in the same voice, suggesting that auditory selective attention can be very efficient.

23

Cherry's (1953) most powerful evidence that people can select one of two auditory messages and ignore the other one came when he questioned the subjects afterwards about their knowledge of the unattended message. Rather surprisingly, most subjects had no awareness of the meaning of the to-be-ignored message, and could not repeat a single word or phrase from it. Some subjects were given a to-be-ignored message in reversed speech. Most of them claimed that the message had been in normal speech, but a few subjects argued that there had been "something queer about it". In spite of their ignorance of the content of the non-shadowed message, most subject were aware of some of its basic physical characteristics, such as the sex of the speaker and the intensity of sound.

Broadbent (1958) was impressed by Cherry's (1953) findings, which influenced the theory of attention that he proposed. According to Broadbent, the information-processing system has limited capacity, and so a filter is required in order to prevent that system from becoming overloaded. More specifically, information about the different stimuli in the environment is initially stored briefly in a sensory buffer. Information about one of the stimuli is then selected for further processing by being allowed to pass through the filter. Information about the other stimuli resides in the sensory buffer for a short period of time, and then decays unless selected by the filter.

Broadbent's (1958) theory provides a neat explanation of Cherry's (1953) main findings. The filter selects one of the two messages on the basis of its physical characteristics (e.g., the ear to which it is presented). The non-shadowed message does not pass through the filter, and thus is not processed in terms of its meaning. However, Cherry's data were limited, in that they were based on subjects who had little familiarity with the shadowing task, and who therefore found it very demanding. The importance of familiarity or practice was demonstrated by Underwood (1974). He asked his subjects to detect digits which were presented in either the shadowed or the non-shadowed message. Unpractised subjects detected only approximately 8 per cent of the digits in the non-shadowed message, whereas a highly practised subject managed to detect 67 per cent of the digits in that message. It is difficult to account for the performance of this subject in terms of a filter which prevents processing of non-shadowed stimuli.

Further problems for filter theory stemmed from the work of Allport, Antonis, and Reynolds (1972). They argued that part of the reason why Cherry's subjects had very little knowledge of the to-be-ignored message was because the shadowed and the non-shadowed messages were both presented in the same sense modality (i.e., auditory), and this caused a certain amount of interference. Allport et al.'s subjects shadowed an auditory message; at the same time some of them attempted to learn either auditorily presented words or pictures. Subsequent memory for the auditorily presented words was extremely poor, whereas there was 90 per cent correct performance on a recognition-memory test for the pictures. Thus, contrary to Broadbent's

(1958) filter theory, two inputs presented at the same time can both be processed thoroughly provided that they are in different sense modalities.

Treisman (1964) responded to some of the problems that were becoming apparent in Broadbent's (1958) theory by proposing an attenuation theory. According to attenuation theory, the processing of unattended auditory inputs is typically attenuated or reduced in comparison with the amount of processing of attended inputs. The major contrast with Broadbent's theory is that the unattended message will generally be processed to some degree. More specifically, Treisman argued that the processing of a message starts with an analysis of its physical characteristics (e.g., loudness, sex of speaker) before proceeding to analyses of grammatical structure and meaning. As a consequence, it is most likely that the physical characteristics of an unattended message will be processed and least likely that its meaning will be processed. This is precisely in line with the findings that Cherry (1953) and others obtained.

A rather different theory of attention was proposed by Deutsch and Deutsch (1963). They argued that attended and unattended inputs are both fully analysed, with one input being selected immediately before a response is made. In other words, the filter or bottleneck to which Broadbent referred is placed considerably later in the processing system than Broadbent himself placed it. It has proved surprisingly difficult to evaluate this theory, but the evidence suggests that it is no more than partially correct (see Eysenck, 1984).

Some theoretical views

Johnston and Heinz (1978) argued that most of the earlier theories of focused auditory attention suffered from the limitation of being too inflexible. Instead of claiming that there is a filter or bottleneck at some particular point in the sequence of processing, it is preferable to think in terms of attentional selectivity occurring at various points depending on the particular task that the subject is carrying out. In general terms, selection of one auditory input occurs as early as possible in processing.

Evidence of flexibility in processing was obtained by Johnston and Wilson (1980). They presented pairs of words at the same time, one member of each pair to each ear. The subjects were instructed to detect members of a specified category (e.g., articles of furniture); these were the targets, and they were all ambiguous words with two quite separate meanings. Each target word was accompanied by a non-target word, which was related either to the appropriate (i.e., category-relevant) meaning of the target, or to its inappropriate (i.e., non-category-relevant) meaning, or was unrelated in meaning to the target. In the focused attention condition, subjects knew which ear the targets would be presented to, whereas they did not know this in the divided attention condition.

The findings are shown in Figure 1. In the focused attention condition, the

25

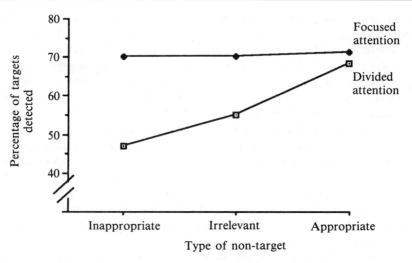

Figure 1   Target detection as a function of attention condition (divided vs. focused)
and of type of non-target
Source: Data from Johnston and Wilson, 1980

relationship between the non-target and target words had no effect on subjects' ability to detect targets. This suggests that the non-target words were
not processed for meaning. In contrast, when subjects did not know where
targets would be presented (i.e., in the divided attention condition), then
target detection was facilitated by appropriate non-targets and reduced by
inappropriate non-targets. This suggests that the non-targets in this condition
were processed for meaning. In other words, there is full processing of all
auditory inputs if this is necessary (as in the divided attention condition), but
this does not happen if it is not necessary (as in the focused attention
condition).

FOCUSED VISUAL ATTENTION

The eye is constructed in such a way that there is a small area of high acuity
in the centre of the retina known as the fovea. The fovea consists solely of
cone cells. These cells are very sensitive, and as a result visual perception is
very clear and precise within the foveal area. However, visual perception is
markedly less clear in the periphery of vision. Here there are only rods, which
permit motion to be detected but not fine details or colour. Psychologists
have argued on the basis of this anatomical evidence that visual perception
resembles a spotlight in that everything in the centre of the spotlight (or in
the foveal area) can be seen with great clarity, but objects lying outside the
beam can be seen imperfectly or not at all. The beams of spotlights are often
adjustable so that the width of the beam can be altered within limits, and it

26

has been suggested (e.g., by LaBerge, 1983) that the same is true of focused visual attention.

The most obvious prediction from the spotlight analogy is that visual stimuli falling within the central area of vision should be processed much more thoroughly than those further away from the central area. Some support for this view was obtained by Johnston and Dark (1985). They gave their subjects the task of identifying a rather unclear test word. They discovered that subjects could identify the test word more easily when a prime word (the same word as the test word or one closely related to it in meaning) was presented to the central visual area immediately before the presentation of the test word. However, identification of the test word was not facilitated when the prime word was presented outside of the central visual area. The implication is that very little information was extracted from the prime word when it was presented outside of the visual attentional spotlight.

The notion that the visual spotlight can be either narrow or broad depending on circumstances was explored by LaBerge (1983). His subjects were shown five-letter words, and had to perform a task which required them to focus on either the entire word or just the middle letter of the word. The evidence indicated that the subjects were able to adjust the breadth of the visual spotlight to make it appropriate for the task in hand.

Feature integration theory

Treisman (1988) proposed an interesting feature integration theory of focused visual attention which built on some of her earlier theoretical views. She started by arguing that there is an important distinction between objects (e.g., a tomato, a tree) and the features of objects (e.g., colour, line, orientations). According to her theory, the features of the objects in the visual environment are processed rapidly and in parallel (i.e., all at the same time), and visual attention is not required for this to happen. In contrast, object perception normally involves integrating the features of a given object (e.g., the roundness and redness of a tomato). This necessitates focused attention and involves a serial (i.e., one at a time) process. In other words, focused attention provides the "glue" which allows us to perceive objects rather than meaningless sets of features.

Some of the evidence leading to this theory was reported by Treisman and Gelade (1980). There was a visual display containing between 1 and 30 items, and the subjects had to decide as rapidly as possible whether a specified target was present. In one condition, the target was the letter S, and so was defined by a single feature. Since only rapid parallel feature processing is required to detect the target in this condition, the number of items in the display should not affect detection time. In a second condition, the target was a green letter T. Since this target is defined by a combination of two features (and can thus be regarded as an object), it should require the serial processing associated

27

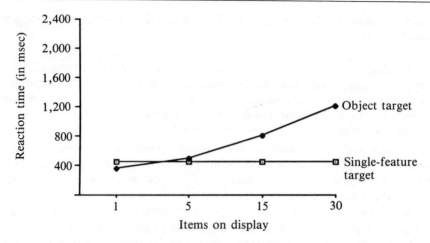

Figure 2 Speed of target detection as a function of target type (single-feature vs. object) and of number of items in the display
Source: Data from Treisman and Gelade, 1980

with focused visual attention. As a consequence, it should take much longer to detect the target when there are several items in the display than when there are only a few.

The findings are shown in Figure 2. It can be seen that performance on the feature-detection task was essentially unaffected by the number of items in the display, whereas performance on the object-detection task was greatly influenced by display size. According to Treisman and Gelade (1980) and Treisman (1988), this difference occurred because focused visual attention was needed on the latter task but not on the former.

Treisman's (1988) feature integration theory has clarified the role of focused visual attention in visual perception. However, as Humphreys and Bruce (1989) pointed out, the theory is in some ways rather oversimplified. More specifically, there are various studies in which subjects were able to identify object targets rapidly without making use of focused attention. What appears to be the case is that feature integration by means of focused attention is needed only when it is relatively difficult to discriminate between the target and non-target stimuli; if the discrimination is easy, then the initial parallel processing of features is adequate.

Inhibitory processes

Our coverage of the processes involved in focused visual attention has been somewhat limited so far, in that we have not considered the possible involvement of inhibitory processes. The position was expressed very well by

28

Wilhelm Wundt (1874), who founded the first laboratory of experimental psychology in 1879:

> The basic phenomenon of all intellectual achievement is the so-called concentration of attention. It is understandable that in the appraisal of this phenomenon we attach importance first and therefore too exclusively to its positive side, to the grasping and clarification of certain presentations. But for the physiological appraisal it is clear that it is the negative side the inhibition of the inflow of all other disturbing excitations ... which is more important. (p. 481)

In spite of Wundt's (1874) statement, it was only comparatively recently that researchers began to investigate inhibitory processes in attention. This research is reviewed by Tipper (1990), who pointed out that there are at least two visual phenomena that demonstrate the existence of inhibitory processes. The first phenomenon concerns the return of attention. If someone's attention is directed to one area of the visual environment and then to another area, it is difficult for that person to detect a target stimulus which is then presented in the first area. It is as if attention is actively inhibited from returning to an area to which it has been directed.

The second phenomenon seems to involve inhibition of the internal representations of objects. For example, a subject is initially presented with two objects at the same time (e.g., a red book and a blue ball), and instructed to name the blue one. If, on a subsequent trial, the subject has to name the previously ignored object (e.g., the red book), he or she performs this task relatively slowly. Presumably the internal representation of a previously ignored object is inhibited, and it is this which slows performance.

Why do these inhibitory processes exist? The first phenomenon makes sense if we assume that it can be important (e.g., in a dangerous environment) to examine the environment in an efficient way without constantly re-inspecting parts of the environment which have just been examined. The second phenomenon makes sense on the basis that inhibitory processes may facilitate the task of ignoring those objects in the environment which are not relevant to our present purposes.

DIVIDED ATTENTION

How good are we at doing two things at once? We know from experience that it is sometimes relatively easy to do and sometimes almost impossible. For example, nearly everyone can combine walking and chewing gum, but it is very difficult to make sense of a book and a television programme at the same time. Psychologists have attempted to identify the factors that determine how successfully attention can be divided between two tasks, and their attempts are considered in this part of the chapter.

There are several everyday examples which demonstrate that the ability to do two things at once depends heavily on practice. Experienced motorists can generally hold a normal conversation while driving, whereas learner drivers find car driving so demanding that they have little or no spare capacity left over to engage in conversation. In similar fashion, expert typists can hold a conversation or listen to the radio while they type, whereas beginning typists cannot.

Experimental evidence that practice can greatly improve the ability to perform two tasks together was obtained by Spelke, Hirst, and Neisser (1976). They carried out a study on two students (Diane and John) who initially found it extremely difficult to read short stories for comprehension while at the same time writing down words from dictation. More specifically, their reading speed was greatly slowed and their handwriting on the dictation task was very poor. After they had been given 30 hours of practice, however, Diane and John had the same reading speed and level of comprehension whether or not they had to take dictation at the same time. In addition, their handwriting on the dictation task had improved.

Spelke et al. (1976) were impressed by the performance of the two students. However, they did notice that the students did not appear to be taking in the meaning of the words that were presented for dictation. For example, when 20 successive words presented for dictation all belonged to the same category, the students did not realize that fact. John and Diane were given additional practice at this aspect of dictation, so that eventually they could write down the names of the categories to which the dictated words belonged while at the same time reading at high speed and with good comprehension.

The finding that reading for comprehension can be successfully combined with dictation suggests that two reasonably complex tasks can be performed together provided that sufficient practice is provided. More support for this contention comes from Shaffer (1975). He discovered that a highly trained typist could type rapidly and accurately while at the same time repeating back or shadowing an auditory message. However, while Shaffer's findings and those of Spelke et al. (1976) and Allport et al. (1972) appear to indicate that there are no problems with performing two well-practised tasks at once, this is not quite true. As Broadbent (1982) pointed out in a review, there are indications that the two tasks interfered with each other to some extent (e.g., increasing the number of errors on the dictation task).

The level of performance under divided attention conditions does not depend only on the extent to which the tasks have been practised. It depends also on the degree of similarity of the two tasks. Tasks can be similar in a number of ways, including having the same modality of input (e.g., visual or auditory), use of common internal processes (e.g., short-term memory), or similar response requirements. Evidence indicating that divided attention suffers when the two tasks are similar in any of these respects was reviewed by Wickens (1984). Here we consider a single example. Kolers (1972) devised a headgear with a half-silvered mirror. When he was wearing this headgear, he could choose whether to see the visual environment in front of him or behind him. However, he could not see both visual environments at the same time, because the one that he was not attending to directly seemed to disappear.

Another factor that determines how well two tasks can be performed together is the difficulty or complexity of the individual tasks. It is almost self-evident that it would be more difficult to combine complex than simple tasks, and only one study will be mentioned to illustrate the point. Earlier in the chapter we considered the dichotic listening task, in which auditory message to one ear has to be repeated back or shadowed at the same time as a second auditory message is presented to the other ear. Sullivan (1976) considered subjects' ability to detect certain words on the non-shadowed message. Many more words were detected when the shadowed message was easy to comprehend than when it was difficult to comprehend.

Theoretical accounts

The simplest way of attempting to account for the findings from studies of divided attention is to assume that there is some very general central capacity or pool of resources such as attention or effort. Each task makes some demands on those resources. If the combined demands of the two tasks exceeds the available pool of resources, then the tasks will interfere with each other and performance will suffer. On the other hand, if the demands of the two for attention or effort fall below the available level of resources, then the two tasks can be performed successfully at the same time.

Such central capacity theories (e.g., Norman & Bobrow, 1975) obviously provide a potential explanation of the effects of task difficulty on performance in studies of divided attention. They can also accommodate the effects of practice, if one assumes that the demands of any given task are much reduced after prolonged practice. However, central capacity theories do not in general provide a good account of the effects of task similarity, as can be seen in the following example. Segal and Fusella (1970) asked their subjects to think of a visual or an auditory image. While they were thinking of this image, they were given the task of attempting to detect either a visual or an auditory signal. The findings are shown in Figure 3. It can be seen that the subjects performed much worse on the auditory signal task when they were thinking about an auditory image than when they were thinking about a visual image. Within the central capacity theory, this suggests that the auditory image task was more demanding of attention or other resources than was the visual image task. However, the results from the visual signal task suggest that the visual image task was more demanding than the auditory image task.

An alternative theoretical approach has been proposed by several theorists (e.g., Eysenck, 1984). In essence, it is proposed that we possess several specific processing mechanisms in addition to a more general processing mechanism such as attention. These specific processing mechanisms all have

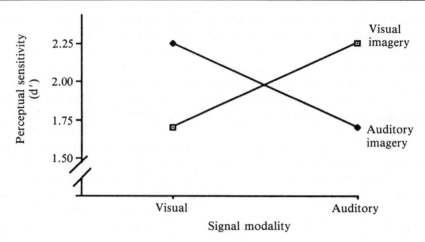

Figure 3 Sensitivity of signal detection as a function of signal modality and of imagery modality
Source: Data from Segal and Fusella, 1970

limited capacity, and may take many different forms. For example, there may be a processing mechanism which is specialized for the processing of auditory information and a different processing mechanism which is specialized for visual information. The reason why performance on the visual signal task is worse when it is combined with visual imagery than with auditory imagery may be because the visual signal task and the visual imagery task together exceed the capacity of the visual processing mechanism. In similar fashion, the auditory signal task and the auditory image task compete for the limited resources of a different specific processing mechanism.

In sum, it is possible to argue that the effects of task difficulty and of practice on dual-task performance are mainly due to the central processor or attentional limitations. In contrast, the effects of task similarity on performance are due to more specific processing mechanisms.

As we have seen, an individual's ability to perform two tasks at the same time can be greatly improved by practice. An important issue here is to identify precisely how practice produces this beneficial effect. According to several theorists (e.g., Logan, 1988; Shiffrin & Schneider, 1977) practice often permits some of the processes involved in task performance to become automatic. There have been disagreements about the definition of an automatic process, but it is generally agreed that automatic processes do not require attention, that they occur rapidly, that they always occur when an appropriate stimulus is presented, and that they do not require conscious awareness. Improved dual-task performance as a result of practice is thought to occur in large measure because of the development of automatic processes which make no demands on attentional resources. Thus, for example, a skilled typist can type and shadow an auditory message at the same time (Shaffer, 1975) because nearly all of the processes involved in typing are automatic, so that there is no need to attend to the movements of the fingers as each letter is typed.

We still do not have a detailed account of how automatic processes develop. However, Logan (1988) has made a start in that direction. He argued that repeated experience with a given stimulus leads to the storage of valuable information about that stimulus and how best to respond to it. In other words, as a result of practice, the appropriate response to a stimulus is stored firmly in memory and can be retrieved very easily. In Logan's own words, "Automaticity is memory retrieval: performance is automatic when it is based on a single-step direct-access retrieval of past solutions from memory" (p. 493).

Logan's (1988) theoretical analysis makes it possible to understand why automatic processes do not require attention, are rapid, and do not involve conscious awareness. They do not require attention because they involve an almost effortless retrieval of well-learned information from memory. They are rapid because the appropriate response is readily accessible in memory. They do not involve conscious awareness because no thought processes intervene between presentation of a stimulus and the retrieval and production of the appropriate response.

ABSENT-MINDEDNESS

According to *Collins English Dictionary*, absent-minded means "preoccupied; forgetful; inattentive", in other words, people are absent-minded when they fail to attend to the task in hand. This common-sense view (which as we shall see has much to recommend it) indicates the value of considering the everyday phenomenon of absent-mindedness in a chapter on attention. Absent-mindedness is often associated with action slips, which involve the performance of unintended actions. There are important reasons for obtaining a good understanding of absent-mindedness in general and action slips in particular: many fatal accidents (e.g., aircraft crashes, workplace deaths) occur as a direct consequence of people's inattention to what they are supposed to be doing.

The most obvious problem that faces the researcher in this area is the difficulty of obtaining adequate numbers of absent-minded actions under laboratory conditions. What is often done is to ask people to keep diary records of any action slips that they detect in their everyday lives. For example, Reason (1979) collected over 400 action slips from 35 individuals, and Reason and Mycielska (1982) managed to obtain a total of 625 action slips from 98 subjects. The most common form of action slip recorded involved storage failure, in which crucial information is forgotten. Here is an example of a storage failure from one of the subjects: "I started to pour a second kettle

of boiling water into a teapot full of freshly made tea. I had no recollection of having just made it" (Reason, 1979, p. 74).

Approximately 40 per cent of all of the action slips recorded by Reason (1979) were storage failures. The next most common category of slips was that of test failure, which accounted for 20 per cent of the action slips. Test failure occurs when the progress of a sequence of planned actions is not attended to adequately at some crucial stage in the sequence. Reason quoted the following example of a test failure "I meant to get my car out, but as I passed through my back porch on my way to the garage I stopped to put on my wellington boots and gardening jacket as if to work in the garden" (p. 73). The other major categories identified by Reason (1979) and by Reason and Mycielska (1982) were subroutine failures, discrimination failures, and programme assembly failures. Subroutine failures occur when there are omissions or re-orderings of the various component stages involved in carrying out a given action sequence. Discrimination failures occur when the individual fails to discriminate accurately between two stimuli (e.g., brushing one's teeth with shaving cream rather than with toothpaste). Finally, programme assembly failures involve inappropriate combinations of actions.

It is important to consider some of the limitations of these diary studies. First, only those action slips that were detected by those keeping the diaries were included. There may have been numerous action slips that were either undetected or not remembered subsequently, and so did not appear in the diaries. That means that no great weight can be attached to the percentage figures for the various categories. Second, the number of times that action slips of a particular kind occur is meaningful only in relation to the number of times on which that kind of action slip might have occurred. For example, there may have been relatively few discrimination failures either because people are very good at discriminating between similar stimuli or because people only rarely find themselves in the position of having to discriminate between confusable stimuli.

There is an apparent paradox about action slips, which mostly occur during the action sequences that have been performed numerous times previously and are thus highly practised. Practice generally leads to considerable improvements in performance and to a marked reduction in the number of errors, and yet with action slips precisely the opposite seems to be the case. Reason (1979) provided a potential explanation for this apparent paradox. According to him, people performing unpractised skills tend to use a closed-loop or feedback mode of control in which a central processor or attentional system guides and controls behaviour from start to finish of an action sequence. However, when people become skilled, they tend to make more use of an open-loop mode of control in which motor performance is under the control of pre-arranged instruction sequences or motor programmes. Use of this open-loop mode of control frees the individual's attentional resources to be used for other purposes. The implications so far as action slips are concerned are as follows:

> The performance of a highly practised and largely automatized job liberates the central processor from moment-to-moment control; but since, like Nature, focal attention abhors a vacuum it tends to be 'captured' by some pressing but parallel mental activity so that, on occasion, it fails to switch back to the task in hand at a 'critical decision point' and thus permits the guidance of action to fall by default under the control of 'strong' motor programmes (p. 85).

The essence of Reason's (1979) theoretical position is that action slips generally occur when we place too much reliance on automatic processes in the open-loop mode of control rather than on attentional processes using the closed-loop or feedback mode of control. It is mainly with practised action sequences that we are in a position to be able to rely on automatic processes, and so most action slips are found when such action sequences are being performed. Most action slips could be avoided if attentional processes or the central processor were to be used continuously during the performance of every action sequence. However, paying full attention to over-learned actions (e.g., walking down a street) would be wasteful of precious processing resources. What most of us do most of the time is to shift rapidly between automatic and attentional processes as and when necessary. That this is a sensible strategy to adopt is suggested by the fact that the diarists studied by Reason (1979) and by Reason and Mycielska (1982) reported an average of only one action slip per day and probably did not make many more slips than that. In other words, the very occasional action slip is a price which is generally well worth paying in order to free the attentional system from the task of constant monitoring of our habitual actions.

VIGILANCE

Most of the research on attention that has been discussed in this chapter has been concerned with reasonably complex tasks which were performed for relatively short periods of time. However, there are various real-life tasks that differ considerably from those we have been discussing. Inspecting goods moving along a conveyor belt in order to detect faulty ones is an example of a task that is monotonous and long-lasting, and on which action is only occasionally required. Tasks possessing such characteristics pose particular problems for the attentional system, because they require continuous attention in a rather boring situation. Performance on monotonous tasks (often called vigilance tasks) has been studied extensively under laboratory conditions in order to determine how successfully subjects can handle the attentional demands such tasks impose.

The first major programme of research on vigilance was reported by Mackworth (1950). He asked his subjects to observe a clock pointer, and to indicate whenever they detected a double jump in the movements of this pointer. One of his major findings was that there was vigilance decrement, meaning that the likelihood of detecting each double jump of the pointer tended to decrease during the course of the experimental session. At an intuitive level, it seems plausible to assume that the vigilance decrement occurred because the subjects became fatigued and unmotivated as the task proceeds. Mackworth obtained some support for this viewpoint. Subjects who were given the stimulant drug amphetamine generally showed little or no evidence of vigilance decrement, presumably because the drug prevented them from feeling tired. In similar fashion, Mackworth also discovered that providing knowledge of results in terms of signals missed and correctly detected largely prevented vigilance decrement. Knowledge of results probably had this beneficial effect because it helped to maintain motivation.

More direct evidence of the importance of motivation to vigilance performance was obtained by Nachreiner (1977). Some of those participating in a vigilance experiment were told that they would be offered a well-paid part-time job if they performed well on the vigilance task, whereas others were not given this inducement. The motivational effects of the job offer were such that it eliminated vigilance decrement.

Why exactly does the vigilance decrement occur in most circumstances? As Broadbent (1971) pointed out, there are two quite different possibilities which need to be considered. First, the subjects may find it increasingly more difficult to attend fully to the task with the consequence that they become less sensitive to the to-be-detected stimuli or signals (e.g., double jumps of the clock pointer). Second, as time goes by the subjects may become more cautious about reporting signals, i.e., they are more reluctant to accept that a signal has been presented. In order to distinguish between these two possibilities it is necessary to take account of what are known as false alarms. These are the occasions on which a signal is reported in spite of the fact that no signal was actually presented. In general terms, subjects who are rather cautious about reporting signals will make fewer false alarms than those who are less cautious. As Broadbent pointed out, the number of false alarms typically declines during the course of a vigilance task. Analyses that take account of the numbers of correct detections and false alarms indicate that the vigilance decrement is due primarily to increased cautiousness in reporting signals rather than to any reduction in the subject's level of sensitivity to signals.

There has been a steady reduction in vigilance research; probably the single most important reason is that it has proved difficult to identify with any precision the changes in attentional functioning which occur during the course of a vigilance experiment. This has made vigilance research of less theoretical significance than had initially been anticipated. Another reason is that technological advances and other changes within society have reduced the number of workers whose jobs involve sitting passively looking out for stimuli that occur only rarely. Many vigilance tasks formerly performed by humans are nowadays performed by computers. As a consequence, vigilance research has lost some of its practical relevance.

FURTHER READING

Eysenck, M. W., & Keane, M. T. (1990). *Cognitive psychology: A student's handbook*. London: Lawrence Erlbaum.
Gopher, D. (1990). Attention. In M. W. Eysenck (Ed.) *The Blackwell dictionary of cognitive psychology* (pp. 23–28). Oxford: Basil Blackwell.
Hampson, P. J. (1989). Aspects of attention and cognitive science. *Irish Journal of Psychology, 10*, 261–275.
Johnston, W. A., & Dark, V. J. (1986). Selective attention. *Annual Review of Psychology, 37*, 43–75.

REFERENCES

Allport, D. A., Antonis, B., & Reynolds, P. (1972). On the division of attention: A disproof of the single channel hypothesis. *Quarterly Journal of Experimental Psychology, 24*, 225–235.
Broadbent, D. E. (1958). *Perception and communication*. Oxford: Pergamon.
Broadbent, D. E. (1971). *Decision and stress*. London: Academic Press.
Broadbent, D. E. (1982). Task combination and selective intake of information. *Acta Psychologica, 50*, 253–290.
Cherry, E. C. (1953). Some experiments on the recognition of speech with one and two ears. *Journal of the Acoustical Society of America, 25*, 975–979.
Deutsch, J. A., & Deutsch, D. (1963). Attention: Some theoretical considerations. *Psychological Review, 70*, 80–90.
Eysenck, M. W. (1984). *A handbook of cognitive psychology*. London: Lawrence Erlbaum.
Humphreys, G. W., & Bruce, V. (1989). *Visual cognition: Computational, experimental and neuropsychological perspectives*. London: Lawrence Erlbaum.
James, W. (1890). *Principles of psychology*. New York: Holt.
Johnston, W A., & Dark, V. J. (1985). Dissociable domains of selective processing. In M. I. Posner & O. S. M. Marin (Eds) *Mechanisms of attention: Attention and performance* (vol. 10, pp. 487–508) Hillsdale, NJ: Lawrence Erlbaum.
Johnston, W. A., & Heinz, S. P. (1978). Flexibility and capacity demands of attention. *Journal of Experimental Psychology: General, 107*, 420–435.
Johnston, W. A., & Wilson, J. (1980). Perceptual processing of non-targets in an attention task. *Memory & Cognition, 8*, 372–377.
Kolers, P. A. (1972). *Aspects of motion perception*. New York: Pergamon.
LaBerge, D. (1983). Spatial extent of attention to letters and words. *Journal of Experimental Psychology: Human Perception and Performance, 9*, 371–379.
Logan, O. D. (1988). Toward an instance theory of automatisation. *Psychological Review, 95*, 492–527.
Mackworth, N. H. (1950). Researches in the measurement of human performance. *Medical Research Council special report series 268*.
Nachreiner, F. (1977). Experiments on the validity of vigilance experiments. In R. R. Mackie (Ed.) *Vigilance: Theory, operational performance and physiological correlates* (pp. 569–592). New York: Plenum.
Norman, D. A., & Bobrow, D. G. (1975). On data-limited and resource-limited processes. *Cognitive Psychology, 7*, 44–64.

Reason, J. T. (1979). Actions not as planned. In G. Underwood & R. Stevens (Eds) *Aspects of consciousness* (pp. 69–96). London: Academic Press.

Reason, J. T., & Mycielska, K. (1982). *Absent-minded? The psychology of mental lapses and everyday errors*. Englewood Cliffs, NJ: Prentice-Hall.

Segal, S. J., & Fusella, V. (1970). Influence of imaged pictures and sounds on detection of visual and auditory signals. *Journal of Experimental Psychology, 83*, 458–464.

Shaffer, L. H. (1975). Multiple attention in continuous verbal tasks. In P. M. A. Rabbitt & S. Dornic (Eds) *Attention and performance* (vol. 5, pp. 243–258). London: Academic Press.

Shiffrin, R. M., & Schneider, W. (1977). Controlled and automatic human information processing: II. Perceptual learning, automatic attending, and a general theory. *Psychological Review, 84*, 127–190.

Spelke, E. S., Hirst, W. C., & Neisser, U. (1976). Skills of divided attention. *Cognition, 4*, 215–230.

Sullivan, L. (1976). Selective attention and secondary message analysis: A reconsideration of Broadbent's filter model of selective attention. *Quarterly Journal of Experimental Psychology, 28*, 167–178.

Tipper, S. P. (1990). Inhibitory processes in attention. In M. W. Eysenck (Ed.) *The Blackwell dictionary of cognitive psychology* (pp. 28–30). Oxford: Basil Blackwell.

Treisman, A. M. (1964). Verbal cues, language, and meaning in selective attention. *American Journal of Psychology, 77*, 206–219.

Treisman, A. M. (1988). Features and objects: The 14th Bartlett Memorial Lecture. *Quarterly Journal of Experimental Psychology, 40A*, 201–237.

Treisman, A. M., & Gelade, G. (1980). A feature-integration theory of attention. *Cognitive Psychology, 12*, 97–136.

Underwood, G. (1974). Moray vs. the rest: The effects of extended shadowing practice. *Quarterly Journal of Experimental Psychology, 26*, 368–372.

Wickens, C. D. (1984). Processing resources in attention. In R. Parasuraman & D. R. Davies (Eds) *Varieties of attention* (pp. 487–516). London: Academic Press.

Wundt, W. (1874). *Grundzüge der physiologischen Psychologie (Principles of physiological psychology)*. Berlin: Springer.

3

PSYCHOLINGUISTICS

Willem J. M. Levelt

Max-Planck-Institut für Psycholinguistik, Nijmegen,
The Netherlands

Conversation	**Speech understanding**
The mental lexicon	Acoustic-phonetic analysis
Speaking	Phonological decoding
Conceptual preparation	Grammatical decoding
Grammatical encoding	Discourse processing
Phonological encoding	**Reading**
Articulation	**Sign language**
Self-monitoring	**Further reading**
	References

Psycholinguistics is the study of the mental processes and skills underlying the production and comprehension of language, and of the acquisition of these skills. This chapter will deal with the former aspect only; for the acquisition of language see the suggested "Further reading" at the end of this chapter.

Although the term "psycholinguistics" was brought into vogue during the 1950s, the psychological study of language use is as old as psychology itself. As early as 1879, for instance, Francis Galton published the first study of word associations (Galton, 1879). And the year 1900 saw the appearance of Wilhelm Wundt's monumental two-volume work *Die Sprache*. It endeavoured to explain the phylogeny of language in the human mind as an increasingly complex and conscious means of expression in a society, and to describe how language is created time and again in the individual act of speaking. Although Wundt deemed it impossible to study language use experimentally, his contemporaries introduced the experimental study of reading (Huey), of

39

verbal memory and word association (Ebbinghaus, Marbe, Watt), and of sentence production (Bühler, Seltz). They began measuring vocabulary size (Binet), and started collecting and analysing speech errors (Meringer and Mayer). The study of neurologically induced language impairments acquired particular momentum after Paul Broca and Carl Wernicke discovered the main speech and language supporting areas in the brain's left hemisphere. In the absence of live brain tomography, aphasiologists began developing neurolinguistic tests for the purpose of localizing brain dysfunctions.

All of these themes persist in modern psycholinguistics. But developments since the 1950s have provided it with two of its most characteristic features, which concern linguistic *processing* and *representation*. With respect to processing, psycholinguistics has followed mainstream psychology in that it considers the language user as a *complex information processing* system. With respect to representation, psycholinguists stress the gigantic amount of *linguistic knowledge* the language user brings to bear in producing and understanding language. Although the structure of this knowledge is the subject matter of linguistics, it is no less a psychological entity than is language processing itself (Chomsky, 1968). Psycholinguistics studies how linguistic knowledge is exploited in language use, how representations for the form and meaning of words, sentences, and texts are constructed or manipulated by the language user, and how the child acquires such linguistic representations.

I shall first introduce the canonical setting for language use: conversation. Next I shall consider the mental lexicon, the heart of our linguistic knowledge. I shall then move to the processes of speaking and speech understanding respectively. Finally I shall turn to other modes of language use, in particular written language and sign language.

CONVERSATION

Our linguistic skills are primarily tuned to the proper conduct of conversation. The innate ability to converse has provided our species with a capacity to share moods, attitudes, and information of almost any kind, to assemble knowledge and skills, to plan coordinated action, to educate its offspring, in short, to create and transmit culture. And all this at a scale that is absolutely unmatched in the animal kingdom. In addition, we converse with ourselves, a kind of autostimulation that makes us more aware of our inclinations, of what we think or intend (Dennett, 1991). Fry (1977) correctly characterized our species as *homo loquens.*

In conversation the interlocutors are involved in negotiating meaning. When we talk, we usually have some kind of communicative intention, and the conversation is felicitous when that intention is recognized by our partner(s) in conversation (Grice, 1968; Sperber & Wilson, 1986). This may take several turns of mutual clarification. Here is an example from Clark and

Wilkes-Gibbs (1986), where subjects had to refer to complex tangram figures:

A: Uh, person putting a shoe on.
B: Putting a shoe on?
A: Uh huh. Facing left. Looks like he's sitting down.
B: Okay.

Here the communicative intention was to establish reference, and that is often a constituting component of a larger communicative goal. Such goals can be to commit the interlocutor or oneself to some course of action, as in requesting and promising, or to inform the interlocutor on some state of affairs, as in asserting, for example. The appropriate linguistic acts for achieving such goals are called *speech acts* (Austin, 1962).

Although what is said is the means of making the communicative intention recognizable, the relation between the two can be highly indirect. Conversations involve intricate mechanisms of politeness control (Brown & Levinson, 1987). What is *conveyed* is often quite different from what is *said*. In most circumstances, for instance, we don't request by commanding, like in "Open the window". Rather we do it indirectly by checking whether the interlocutor is able or willing to open the window, like in "Can you open the window for me?" It would, then, be inappropriate for the interlocutor to answer "Yes" without further action. In that case, the response is only to the question (whether he or she is able to open the window), but not to the request.

How does the listener know that there is a request in addition to the question? There is, of course, an enormous amount of shared situational knowledge that will do the work. Grice (1975) has argued that conversations are governed by principles of rationality; Sperber and Wilson (1986) call it the *principle of relevance*. The interlocutor, for instance, is so obviously able to open the window that the speaker's intention cannot have been to check that ability. But Clark (1979) found that linguistic factors play a role as well. If the question is phrased idiomatically, involving *can* and *please*, subjects interpret it as a request. But the less idiomatic it is (like in "Are you able to ..."), the more subjects react to the question instead of to the request.

Another important aspect of conversation is *turn-taking*. There are rules for the allocation of turns in conversation that ensure everybody's right to talk, that prevent the simultaneous talk of different parties, and that regulate the proper engaging in and disengaging from conversation (Sacks, Schegloff, & Jefferson, 1974). These rules are mostly followed, and sometimes intentionally violated (as in interrupting the speaker). Turn-taking is subtly controlled by linguistic (especially prosodic) and non-verbal (gaze and body movement) cues (Beattie, 1983).

THE MENTAL LEXICON

Producing or understanding spoken language always involves the use of

41

words. The mental lexicon is our repository of words, their meanings, their syntax, and their sound forms. A language's vocabulary is, in principle, unlimited in size. Take, for instance, the numerals in English. They alone form an infinite set of words. But it is unlikely that a word such as *twenty-three-thousand-two-hundred-and-seventy-nine* is an entry in our mental lexicon. Rather, such a word is constructed by rule when needed. We have the ability to produce new words that are not stored in our mental lexicon.

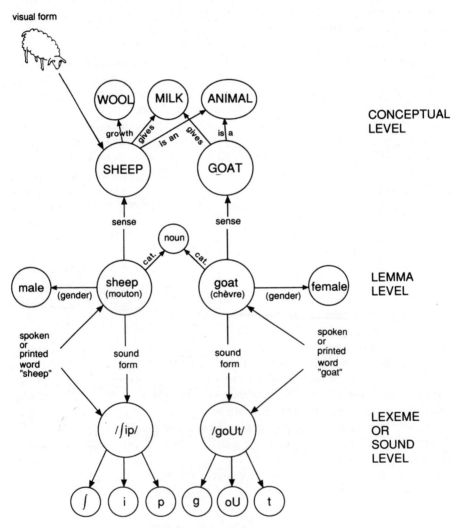

Figure 1   Fragment of a lexical network. Each word is represented at the conceptual, the syntactic and the sound form level
Source: Bock and Levelt, 1993

How many words *are* stored? Miller (1991) estimates that the average high school graduate knows about 60,000 words (under one definition of "word").

One way of representing this enormous body of knowledge is by way of network models. Figure 1 shows a fragment of such a network. Each word is represented by three nodes, one at the conceptual level, one at the syntactic (grammatical) or lemma level, and one at the sound form (phonological) or lexeme level. The lemma is the syntactic representation and the lexeme is the phonological representation. A word's semantic properties are given by its connections to other nodes at the conceptual level (for instance, that a sheep is an animal, gives milk, etc.). A word's syntactic properties are represented by its lemma node's relations to other syntactic nodes (for instance, "sheep" is a noun; French "mouton" has male gender, etc.). The sound form properties, finally, such as a word's phonological segments, are represented in the way a word's lexeme node relates to other sound form nodes ("sheep" for instance contains three ordered phonological segments, $/ʃ/$, $/i/$, and $/p/$, as shown in Figure 1).

Different authors have proposed different network models (e.g., Collins & Loftus, 1975; Dell, 1986; Roelofs, 1992), and for different purposes. It is unlikely that such networks can adequately represent all complexities of our semantic, syntactic, and phonological knowledge about words. But they can be useful in predicting speed of word access in comprehension and production, as well as in explaining various kinds of errors that we make in speech production and various disorders of accessing words in aphasic speech.

Especially important for theories of language use are the ways that verbs are represented in the mental lexicon. As a semantic entity, a verb assigns semantic roles to its arguments. The verb *walk*, for instance, requires an animate argument that specifies the role of agent, as in *John walked*. The verb *greet* governs two arguments, one for the agent and one for the recipient of the action, as in *Peter greeted the driver*. As a syntactic entity, a verb assigns syntactic functions to the sentence constituents it governs. In the above sentence, *Peter* is the subject and *the driver* the object. A verb's argument-function mapping is not random. Most verbs, for instance, map a recipient argument on to a syntactic object function, but not all. The verb *receive* doesn't. In *Mary received the book*, *Mary* is both recipient and sentence subject. Also, verbs often allow for multiple mappings. In *the driver was greeted by Peter*, the recipient, not the agent appears in subject position.

For each verb, the mental lexicon contains its possible mapping frames. These play an important role in the speaker's syntactic planning and in the listener's syntactic and semantic parsing.

SPEAKING

Speaking is our most complex cognitive-motor skill. It involves the conception of an intention, the selection of information whose expression will make that intention recognizable, the selection of appropriate words, the construction of a syntactic framework, the retrieval of the words' sound forms, and the computation of an articulatory plan for each word and for the utterance as a whole. It also involves the execution of this plan by more than 100 muscles controlling the flow of air through the vocal tract. Finally, it involves a process of self-monitoring by which speech trouble can be prevented or repaired. The following is a bird eye's view over these processes.

Conceptual preparation

The question where communicative intentions come from is a psychodynamic question rather than a psycholinguistic one. Speaking is a form of social action, and it is in the context of action that intentions, goals, and subgoals develop. It is not impossible, though, that the intention *what* to say occasionally arises from spontaneous activity in the speech formulating system itself. It can create rather incoherent "internal speech", which we can self-perceive. This, in turn, may provide us with tatters of notions that we then consider for expression (cf. Dennett, 1991).

Conveying an intention may involve several steps or "speech acts". The speaker will have to decide what to express first, what next, and so on. This is called the speaker's *linearization* problem (Levelt, 1989). It is especially apparent in the expression of multidimensional information, as in describing one's apartment (Linde & Labov, 1975). The conceptual preparation of speech, and in particular linearization, require the speaker's continuing attention. The principles of linearization are such that attentional load is minimized.

Each speech act, be it a request to do X, an assertion that Y, etc., involves the expression of some conceptual structure, technically called a "message" (Garrett, 1975). That message is to be given linguistic shape; it has to become "formulated".

Grammatical encoding

A first step in formulating is to retrieve the appropriate words from the mental lexicon and to embed them in the developing syntactic structure. In normal conversation we produce some two words per second. At this rate we manage to access the appropriate words in our huge mental lexicon. Occasional errors of lexical selection (such as "Don't burn your toes" where *fingers* was intended) show that the lexicon has a semantic organization.

The standard explanation for such errors is that activation spreads through a semantically organized network, as in Figure 1. In such a network, each node has an activation level between 0 and 1. When the lexical concept node SHEEP is active, then activation spreads to semantically related concept nodes, such as GOAT. Both nodes spread activation "down" to their lemma

44

nodes. Which one of the lemmas will then be selected for further processing? Normally it will be the most activated one, in this case the lemma for "sheep". But the occurrence of an occasional error shows that there is a small probability that a less activated lemma gets selected. According to one theory (Roelofs, 1992) the probability that a particular lemma becomes selected within a time interval t is the ratio of its activation to the sum of the activation of all other lemma nodes. For instance, if "sheep" and "goat" are the only two active lemmas during interval t after presentation of the picture, and they have activation levels of 0.7 and 0.1 respectively, the probability that the target word "sheep" will be selected during that interval is 7/8, whereas the erroneous word "goat" will be selected with the probability 1/8. Hence, if there is more than one lemma active in the system, there is always a small probability that a non-intended word becomes selected (and it is likely to be semantically related to the target).

Spreading activation theories of lexical selection are typically tested in picture-naming experiments, where naming latencies are measured. For a review of issues in lexical selection, see Levelt (1992a).

As soon as a lemma is retrieved, its syntactic properties become available. Among them are the lemma's grammatical class (preposition, noun, verb, etc.). Each lemma requires its own specific syntactic environment or "frame". Syntactic planning is like solving a set of simultaneous equations. Each lemma's frame has to fit its neighbour's frames, and since Garrett (1975) there are theories about how this is realized (see Levelt, 1989, for a review). Actually, the equations are not quite "simultaneous"; the lemmas for an utterance are typically not concurrently retrieved. Lemmas for salient concepts, such as animate objects, tend to be retrieved faster than for non-salient concepts (Bock & Warren, 1985), and that affects their position in the developing syntactic structure. For a review of grammatical encoding, see Bock and Levelt (1994).

Phonological encoding

A selected lemma (but only a selected one: see Levelt et al., 1991) spreads its activation to its lexeme node (cf. Figure 1). At this level two kinds of phonological information become available. The first one is the word's segments, which are "spelled out" one after another. The second one is the word's metrical structure. For "sheep" it is the information that it is a one-syllable word. For "father" it is the information that it is a two-syllabic trochaic word. The metrical frames of successive words are often combined, creating so-called phonological word frames. In *Peter gave him it*, the last three words form one phonological word *gavimit*. In a process of *segment-to-frame association* spelled-out segments are inserted one by one into the corresponding phonological word frames. It is during this ordered insertion that phonological syllables are created, one after another (such as *ga-vi-mit*; see

Levelt, 1992b). How this string of phonological syllables determines the precise articulatory gestures to be made by the speech organs is still a matter of much debate (see especially Browman & Goldstein, 1991).

The notion that segments and frames are independently retrieved arose in the analysis of phonological speech errors (Dell, 1986; Shattuck-Hufnagel, 1979). Spoonerisms such as *with this wing I thee red*, or *fool the pill* (instead of *fill the pool*) show that segments can become associated to the right place in the wrong frame.

Phonological encoding also involves the planning of larger units than phonological words. There is, in particular, the planning of intonational phrases. These are units that carry a particular intonational contour. Such contours can be rising, falling or combinations thereof. They often express a speaker's attitude towards what is said: doubt, certainty, or towards the interlocutor: reassuringness, inviting reaction. See Levelt (1989) for a review of phonological encoding.

The output of phonological encoding is an articulatory programme. Phenomenologically, it appears to the speaker as internal speech. This internal speech need not be articulated. It can be kept in an articulatory buffer, ready to be retrieved for articulatory execution (Sternberg, Wright, Knoll, & Monsell, 1980).

Articulation

The articulatory apparatus consists of three major structures. The respiratory system controls the steady outflow of air from the lungs. The breathing cycle during speech is quite different from normal breathing, with very rapid inhalation and very slow exhalation. The laryngeal system has the vocal cords as its central part. It is the main source of acoustic energy. The vocal tract, finally, contains the cavities of pharynx, mouth, and nose. They are the resonators that filter the acoustic energy in frequency bands or *formants*. Vowels are characterized by their formant structure. The vocal tract can be constricted at different places, and these constrictions can be made or released in different manners. In this way a wide range of consonantal and other speech sounds can be made.

The control of this utterly complex motor system has been the subject of much research. Present theories converge on the notion of *model-referenced control* (Arbib, 1981; see also Figure 2). The motor system is given an "articulatory task" (as part of the articulatory programme), such as "close the lips". There are usually many degrees of freedom in executing such a task. For instance, lip closing can be realized by moving the lips, by moving the jaw, or by doing both to various degrees. The internal model computes the least energy-consuming way of reaching the goal, given the actual state of the articulators (there is continuous proprioceptive feedback to the internal model). The output is a set of efferent control signals to the relevant

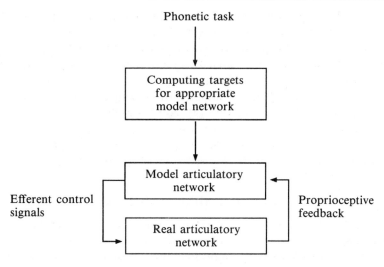

Figure 2 Model-referenced control in articulation
Source: Levelt, 1989

muscles. Saltzman and Kelso (1987) gave a precise mathematical rendering of this theory. See Levelt (1989) for a review of theories of articulation. The output of articulation is overt speech.

Self-monitoring

We can listen to our own overt speech and detect trouble, just as we can listen to the speech of others and detect errors or infelicitous delivery. This involves our normal speech understanding system. We can also detect trouble in our internal speech. When the trouble is disruptive enough for the ongoing conversation, a speaker may decide to interrupt the flow of speech and to make a self-repair.

Not all self-produced trouble (such as errors of selection) is detected by the speaker. Self-monitoring requires attention; we mostly attend to *what* we say, far less to *how* we do it. Detection of trouble is better towards the end of clauses, where less attention for content is required (Levelt, 1989). There are two main classes of trouble that induce repairing. The first one is an all-out error (as in *and above that a horizon-, no a vertical line*); the error can be lexical, syntactic, or phonological. The second one is that something is not really appropriate (as in *to the right is blue – is a blue point*). The speaker then repairs in order to make the utterance more precise, less ambiguous. Upon detecting either kind of trouble, the speaker can self-interrupt. And this ignores linguistic structure; a speaker can stop in the midst of a phrase, a word, or a syllable. But then, the speaker often marks the kind of trouble by some *editing expression*: "no", "sorry", "I mean", for errors; "rather", "that is", for something inappropriate.

Restarting, that is, making the repair proper, is linguistically quite principled. The speaker grafts the repair on to the syntax of the interrupted utterance, which has been kept in abeyance. As a consequence, repairing is like linguistic coordination. One seldom finds a repair such as *is she driving – she walking downtown?* And indeed, the corresponding coordination *is she driving or she walking downtown?* is ill-formed. But *is he – she walking downtown?* is a very common repair type, and it corresponds to a well-formed coordination: *is he or she walking downtown?* (Levelt, 1989).

SPEECH UNDERSTANDING

The canonical objective in speech understanding is to recognize the speaker's communicative intention. How does the listener induce that intention from the speaker's overt speech, a continuous flow of acoustic events?

Several component processes are involved here. First, there is the hearer's acoustic-phonetic analysis of the speech signal, that is, representing it as a *phonetic* not just an *acoustic* event. Second, there is phonological decoding, in particular finding the words that correspond to the phonetic events, and analysing the overall prosodic structure of the utterance. Third, there is grammatical decoding, parsing the utterance as a meaningful syntactic structure. Finally, there is discourse processing, interpreting the utterance in the context of the ongoing discourse, and in particular inferring the speaker's intentions. Let us review these processes in turn.

Acoustic-phonetic analysis

It is very hard, if not impossible, to listen to speech as if it were just a string of chirps, buzzes, hums, and claps. We just cannot help perceiving it as speech. In this so-called "speech mode" (Liberman & Mattingly, 1985) we interpret the acoustic event as resulting from a speaker's articulatory gestures as a phonetic event. There is no unanimity in the literature, though, about what kind of representation the listener derives. According to Liberman and Mattingly, the listener derives the speaker's intended articulatory gestures (even if they were sloppy). Others argue that listeners have special detectors for distinctive events in the speech signal, such as for onsets, for spectral peaks, for the frequencies and motions of formants. The detection of such acoustic events may suffice to derive the presence or absence of phonetic features, such as voicing, nasality, vowel height, stridency, and so on (Stevens & Blumstein, 1981).

Speech segments, clusters, and syllables have characteristic distributions of phonetic features. Hence, if such feature detectors are reliable, they may provide sufficient information for effective phonological decoding. Opinions differ, however, about their reliability. The speech signal is highly variable, dependent as it is on speech rate, sex of the speaker, sloppiness of speech delivery, reverberation or noise in the room, for example. Even if the listener can partial out such effects of the speech context, acoustic-phonetic analysis will often be indeterminate. Still, it may well be sufficient for the purpose. Not every word has to be recognized in order to derive the speaker's intentions. And where a really critical word is missed, the interlocutor will say "what?" or signal difficulty of understanding in other ways.

For an excellent review of acoustic-phonetic processing, see Pisoni and Luce (1987).

Phonological decoding

Whatever the precise character of the phonetic representations, they are the listener's access codes to the mental lexicon. How does a listener recognize words in connected speech? A major problem here is to *segment* the speech, to find out where words begin and end in the continuous flow of speech. There are, basically, two routes here.

The first one is the bottom-up approach, that is, to build on cues in the phonetic representation. Cutler (1990) has argued that English listeners will, by default, segment speech such that there are word boundaries right before stressed syllables. It is a statistical fact of English that 85 per cent of the meaningful words that one encounters while listening begin with a stressed syllable. The segmentation strategy will, therefore, be quite successful. Cutler's theory has meanwhile found substantial experimental support. Also, there are speech sounds that tend to occur at the ends of words, such as [-ng] and [-nd] for English. Speakers may use such phonotactic properties of their language to predict word boundaries.

The second route is top-down. We often recognize a word before it ends. But that means that we can predict the word's end, and hence the upcoming word boundary. That gives us a handle on where to start recognizing the subsequent word.

Given that we know a word's beginning, how do we recognize it? According to the *cohort theory* (Marslen-Wilson, 1989), a small word-initial feature pattern (corresponding to about two segments of the input word) activates all words in the mental lexicon that match it phonologically. Assume the input word is *trespass*, and the cluster [tr] has become available. This will activate all words beginning with [tr], such as *tremble, trespass, trestle, trombone*, etc. This is called the "word-initial cohort". As more phonetic information becomes available, the cohort is successively reduced. When the vowel [ɛ] is perceived, all items not sharing that vowel, such as *trombone*, are deactivated. This process continues until a single candidate remains. For *trespass* this happens when [p] is reached. The segment [p] is, therefore, called the *uniqueness point* of *trespass*. A word's uniqueness point depends on its word-initial lexical alternatives. For most words the uniqueness point precedes the word's end.

For an optimally efficient system, the word's uniqueness point would also be its *recognition point*. There is good experimental evidence in support of this hypothesis (e.g., Frauenfelder, Segui, & Dijkstra, 1990), though the recognition point may slightly anticipate the uniqueness point in case syntactic or semantic information disambiguates the item from its remaining alternatives (Zwitserlood, 1989). Hence, it will often be possible for a listener to anticipate the upcoming word boundary.

Phonological decoding serves not only the recognition of words, but also their groupings into prosodic constituents, such as phonological and intonational phrases. These constituents carry important information about the syntax of the utterance, and about the communicative intentions of the speaker (cf. Levelt, 1989).

Grammatical decoding

As words are successively recognized and prosodically grouped, the listener will as much as possible interpret these materials "on-line" (Marslen-Wilson & Tyler, 1980). Each recognized word makes available its syntactic and semantic properties. There is, then, concurrent syntactic parsing and semantic interpretation, each following its own principles, but interacting where necessary.

In this connection, one should distinguish between local and global syntactic parsing. Local parsing involves the creation of local phrase structure, combining words into noun phrases, verb phrases, etc. There is increasing evidence that local parsing can run on word category information alone (Frazier, 1989; Tyler & Warren, 1987). We have little trouble parsing "jabberwocky" or semantically anomalous prose such as *the beer slept the slow guitar*. Here we construct phrase structure exclusively by recognizing the words' syntactic categories (Art, Adj, N, V). However, successful local parsing is highly dependent on the intactness of phonological phrases, as Tyler and Warren (1987) could show. For instance, in the above anomalous prose, one should not create a prosodic break between *the* and *slow*, or between *slow* and *guitar*.

Global syntactic parsing, however, interacts with semantic interpretation. In global parsing, semantic roles are assigned to syntactic constituents, and this is to a large extent governed by the verb's argument/function mapping. When the meaning of words or phrases contradicts the semantic roles they should carry, global parsing is hampered (Tyler & Warren, 1987).

One important aspect of global parsing is the resolution of anaphora. In the sentence *the boxer told the skier that the doctor for the team would blame him for the recent injury*, the anaphor *him* can refer back to *the boxer* and to *the skier*, but global syntax prohibits its referring to *the doctor*. Indeed, experimental evidence shows reactivation of both *boxer* and *skier*, but not of *doctor* when the pronoun *him* is perceived. Such reactivation can also be measured for so-called null-anaphors as in *the policeman saw the boy that the crowd at the party accused t of the crime*. Here there is measurable reactivation of *boy* at position *t* (the syntactic "trace" of *the boy*; see Nicol & Swinney, 1989). But also in this respect global parsing is semantically facilitated, for instance if the anaphor's referent is a concrete noun (Cloitre & Bever, 1988).

Grammatical decoding doesn't remove all ambiguity (for instance, the pronoun *him* above is not fully resolved). Here, further discourse processing is needed.

Discourse processing

Partners in conversation construct mental models of the state of affairs they are talking about (Johnson-Laird, 1983; Seuren, 1985). Indefinite expressions (such as in *there is a dog in the room*) make them introduce a new entity (a dog) in the model. Definite expressions (such as *the room* in the same sentence) make them look up an already existing entity. The new information in the utterance is then attached to whichever entity it concerns.

Identifying referents is a major accomplishment of human language processing, still unmatched by any computer program. The problem is that referring expressions can be highly indirect. How can a waitress in a restaurant interpret the referent when her colleague says *the hamburger wants the bill*? Nunberg (1979) argued that there are "referring functions" that map a *demonstratum* (like the hamburger) on to the intended referent (the person who ordered it). But the range of possible referring functions is almost unlimited. Clark, Schreuder, and Buttrick (1983) and Morrow (1986) have argued (and experimentally shown) that such demonstratum-to-referent mapping depends on the mutual knowledge of the interlocutors and on the saliency of entities in their discourse models.

Indirectness is the hallmark of discourse interpretation. As mentioned above, what is said often relates quite indirectly to what the speaker intends to convey. It is not only politeness that governs such indirectness. All figures of speech, whether polite or not, require the listener to build a bridge from the literal to the intended. This holds equally for metaphor (Sperber & Wilson, 1986), irony (Clark & Gerrig, 1984), and hyperbole (Grice, 1975).

Finally, whereas acoustic-phonetic, phonological, and grammatical decoding are largely automatic processes, discourse processing requires the listener's full attention. In that respect, it is on a par with the speaker's conceptual preparation. As interlocutors we are concerned with content. The processing of form largely takes care of itself.

READING

The invention of writing systems, whether logographic, syllabic, or alphabetic, is probably the most revolutionary step in human cultural evolution. It added a powerful means of storing and transmitting information. With the invention of printing, it became a major mechanism for large-scale dissemination of knowledge in a culture.

But equally surprising as this ability to map spoken language on to a visual code is our capacity to efficiently process such a code. When skilled, we silently read five or six printed words per second; this is about twice the rate of conversational speech. This ability has not given us any selective advantage in biological evolution; the invention of writing systems is as recent as about 5,000 years ago. Rather, the ability to read must be due to a happy coincidence of other pre-existing faculties of mind.

One of these is, of course, language. As readers we largely use our parsing potential for spoken language. Visual word recognition feeds into the lemma level of Figure 1. As lemmas are successively activated by the printed words, further syntactic, semantic, and discourse processing operates roughly as for spoken language. There are, admittedly, differences too. There is, for instance, no prosody to help syntactic parsing; instead there is punctuation. Also, there is no external enforcement of rate as there is in speech perception.

Another pre-existing faculty on which reading is parasitic is our enormous ability to scan for small meaningful visual patterns. In a hunter's society these were probably animal silhouettes, footprints, and so on. Words (if not too long or too infrequent) are recognized as wholes; a skilled reader processes a word's letters in parallel. Much ink has been spilled on the question whether the letters individually or the word as a whole activate a phonological code in silent reading, that is, the word's lexeme (see Figure 1). Such phonological recoding indeed exists. But it is only for low-frequent words that this "phonological route" is of any help in lemma access (Jared & Seidenberg, 1991). However, this silent "internal speech" probably does play a role in further syntactic and semantic parsing; it is a way of buffering successive words for further processing.

The ability to scan is optimally used in reading. The basic cycle is this: the reader fixates a word for, on average, one-fifth of a second. The fixation is roughly between the beginning and the middle of the word. During this period lexical access is achieved. In addition, there is some perception of the next word in the periphery of vision. Sometimes this suffices to recognize that next word as well on the same fixation (but the fixation will then last somewhat longer). Usually, however, the information from the periphery of vision is used only to plan a saccadic eye movement (a jump of the eye) to that next word. The size of the saccade depends on the length of the next word; the average saccade is about eight characters in size. The new word is fixated, and the cycle starts all over again.

When a word is quite infrequent, or when the reader has trouble integrating it in the developing syntax or semantics, the fixation duration can be substantially longer. Also, the reader may backtrack and refixate an earlier word when there is serious trouble in comprehension.

For a major review of the reading process and its disorders, see Rayner and Pollatsek (1989).

SIGN LANGUAGE

Contrary to written language, the sign languages of deaf people are not parasitic on spoken language. They are autonomous languages in the visual mode. Their mere existence shows that our faculty of language is not crucially

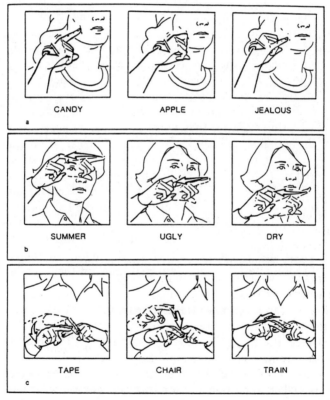

Illustration, copyright Ursula Bellugi, Salk Institute for Biological Studies, La Jolla, CA, 92037

Figure 3 Minimal contrasts between signs in American Sign Language: (a) hand configuration, (b) place of articulation, (c) movement
Source: From Klima and Bellugi, 1979

53

dependent on our ability to speak. Deaf children who grow up in a signing deaf community acquire their language at the same age and in roughly the same stages as hearing children do.

Just as words, signs have form and meaning. The articulators of sign language are the hands, the face, and the body. Where words contrast phonemically (for instance in voicing: *bath* vs *path*), signs contrast in hand configuration, in place of articulation and in hand movement (see Figure 3). Also, facial features may distinguish between signs.

Although the first coining of a sign is often iconic, its meaning is eventually independent of its form, as it is for words in spoken languages. As a consequence, sign languages are mutually unintelligible, just as spoken languages are (contrary to what Wundt suggested in *Die Sprache* − see above).

Sign languages are rich in morphology (for inflection and for derivation of new signs) and have full-fledged recursive syntax. Many syntactic devices are spatial in character. Anaphora, that is, referring back to an earlier introduced entity, is done by pointing to the locus in the signing space (in front of the body) where the original referent was first "established". In American Sign Language the sign for transitive verbs either moves from subject to object locus, or from object to subject locus. Each verb has its own "mapping function" (like in spoken language, see above). For the structure and use of British Sign Language, see Kyle and Woll (1985).

There is increasing evidence that a sign language is subserved by the same areas of the brain that sustain spoken language. Poizner, Klima, and Bellugi, (1987) showed that damage to anterior areas of the left hemisphere in native signers resulted in a style of signing highly comparable to the agrammatism of so-called Broca's patients. Similarly, a form of fluent aphasia resulted when the damage was in a more posterior area of the left hemisphere, comparable to the fluent aphasia of so-called Wernicke's patients. Damage in the right hemisphere left the signing intact, but patients lost the ability to sign coherently *about* spatial relations, such as the layout of their apartment. Their spatial representations were damaged, but not their spatial language.

FURTHER READING

Garman, M. (1990). *Psycholinguistics*. Cambridge: Cambridge University Press.

Levelt, W. J. M. (1989). *Speaking: From intention to articulation*. Cambridge, MA: Massachusetts Institute of Technology Press.

Miller, G. A. (1991). *The science of words*. New York: Scientific American Library.

Rayner, K., & Pollatsek, A. (1989). *The psychology of reading*. Englewood Cliffs, NJ: Prentice-Hall.

Slobin, D. I. (Ed.) (1985). *The crosslinguistic study of language acquisition* (2 vols). Hillsdale, NJ: Lawrence Erlbaum.

REFERENCES

Arbib, M. A. (1981). Perceptual structures and distributed motor control. In V. Brooks (Ed.) *Handbook of physiology: The nervous system. Motor control* (vol. 2, pp. 1449–1480). Bethesda, MD: American Physiological Society.

Austin, J. L. (1962). *How to do things with words.* Oxford: Clarendon.

Beattie, G. (1983). *Talk: An analysis of speech and non-verbal behaviour in conversation.* Milton Keynes: Open University Press.

Bock, J. K., & Levelt, W. J. M. (1994). Language production: Grammatical encoding. In M. A. Gernsbacher (Ed.) *Handbook of psycholinguistics.* New York: Academic Press.

Bock, J. K., & Warren, R. K. (1985). Conceptual accessibility and syntactic structure in sentence formulation. *Cognition, 21,* 47–67.

Browman, C. P., & Goldstein, L. (1991). Representation and reality: Physical systems and phonological structure. *Haskins Laboratory Status Report on Speech Research,* SR-105/106, 83–92.

Brown, P., & Levinson, S. (1987). *Politeness: Some universals in language usage.* Cambridge: Cambridge University Press.

Chomsky, N. (1968). *Language and mind.* New York: Harcourt Brace & World.

Clark, H. H. (1979). Responding to indirect speech acts. *Cognitive Psychology, 4,* 430–477.

Clark, H. H., & Gerrig, R. J. (1984). On the pretence theory of irony. *Journal of Experimental Psychology: General, 113,* 121–126.

Clark, H. H., & Wilkes-Gibbs, D. (1986). Referring as a collaborative process. *Cognition, 22,* 1–39.

Clark, H. H., Schreuder, R., & Buttrick, S. (1983). Common ground and the understanding of demonstratives. *Journal of Verbal Learning and Verbal Behavior, 22,* 245–258.

Cloitre, M., & Bever, T. G. (1988). Linguistic anaphors, levels of representation, and discourse. *Language and Cognitive Processes 3,* 293–322.

Collins, A. M., & Loftus, E. F. (1975). A spreading-activation theory of semantic processing. *Psychological Review, 82,* 407–428.

Cutler, A. (1990). Exploiting prosodic probabilities in speech segmentation. In G. Altmann (Ed.) *Cognitive models of speech processing* (pp. 105–121). Cambridge, MA: Massachusetts Institute of Technology Press.

Dell, G. (1986). A spreading activation theory of retrieval in sentence production. *Psychological Review, 93,* 283–321.

Dennett, D. C. (1991). *Consciousness explained.* Boston, MA: Little, Brown.

Frauenfelder, U., Segui, J., & Dijkstra, T. (1990). Lexical effects in phoneme processing: Facilitatory or inhibitory? *Journal of Experimental Psychology: Human Perception and Performance, 16,* 77–91.

Frazier, L. (1989). Against lexical generation. In W. D. Marslen-Wilson (Ed.) *Lexical representation and process* (pp. 505–528). Cambridge, MA: Massachusetts Institute of Technology Press.

Fry, D. (1977). *Homo loquens.* Cambridge: Cambridge University Press.

Galton, F. (1879). Psychometric experiments. *Brain, 2,* 149–162.

Garrett, M. F. (1975). An analysis of sentence production. In G. Bower (Ed.) *Psychology of learning and motivation* (vol. 9, pp. 133–177). New York: Academic Press.

Grice, H. P. (1968). Utterer's meaning, sentence meaning and word meaning. *Foundations of Language, 4,* 225–242.

Grice, H. P. (1975). Some further notes on logic and conversation. In P. Cole (Ed.) *Syntax and semantics: Pragmatics* (vol. 9, pp. 113–127). New York: Academic Press.

Jared, D., & Seidenberg, M. S. (1991). Does word identification proceed from spelling to sound to meaning? *Journal of Experimental Psychology: General, 120,* 358–394.

Johnson-Laird, P. N. (1983). *Mental models.* Cambridge: Cambridge University Press.

Klima, E. S., & Bellugi, U. (1979). *The signs of language.* Cambridge, MA: Harvard University Press.

Kyle, J. G., & Woll, B. (1985). *Sign language.* Cambridge: Cambridge University Press.

Levelt, W. J. M. (1989). *Speaking: From intention to articulation.* Cambridge, MA: Massachusetts Institute of Technology Press.

Levelt, W. J. M. (Ed.) (1992a). Lexical access in speech production. Special issue of *Cognition, 42,* 1–316.

Levelt, W. J. M. (1992b). Accessing words in speech production: Stages, processes and representations. *Cognition, 42,* 1–22.

Levelt, W. J. M., Schriefers, H., Vorberg, D., Meyer, A. S., Pechmann, T., & Havinga, J. (1991). The time course of lexical access in speech production: A study of picture naming. *Psychological Review, 98,* 122–142.

Liberman, A. M., & Mattingly, I. G. (1985). The motor theory of speech perception revised. *Cognition, 21,* 1–36.

Linde, C., & Labov, W. (1975). Spatial networks as a site for the study of language and thought. *Language, 51,* 924–939.

Marslen-Wilson, W. (1989). Access and integration: Projecting sound onto meaning. In W. D. Marslen-Wilson (Ed.) *Lexical representation and process* (pp. 3–24). Cambridge, MA: Massachusetts Institute of Technology Press.

Marslen-Wilson, W., & Tyler, L. (1980). The temporal structure of spoken language understanding. *Cognition, 8,* 1–71.

Miller, G. A. (1991). *The science of words.* New York: Scientific American Library.

Morrow, D. G. (1986). Places as referents in discourse. *Journal of Memory and Language, 25,* 676–690.

Nicol, J., & Swinney, D. (1989). The role of structure in coreference assignment during sentence comprehension. *Journal of Psycholinguistic Research, 18,* 5–19.

Nunberg, G. (1979). The non-uniqueness of semantic solutions: Polysemy. *Linguistics and Philosophy, 3,* 143–184.

Pisoni, D. B., & Luce, P. A. (1987). Acoustic-phonetic representations in word recognition. *Cognition, 25,* 21–52.

Poizner, H., Klima, E. S., & Bellugi, U. (1987). *What the hands reveal about the brain.* Cambridge, MA: Massachusetts Institute of Technology Press.

Rayner, K., & Pollatsek, A. (1989). *The psychology of reading.* Englewood Cliffs, NJ: Prentice-Hall.

Roelofs, A. (1992). A spreading-activation theory of lemma retrieval in speaking. *Cognition, 42,* 107–142.

Sacks, H., Schegloff, E. A., & Jefferson, G. (1974). A simplest systematics for the organization of turn-taking in conversation. *Language, 50,* 696–735.

Saltzman, E., & Kelso, J. A. S. (1987). Skilled action: A task-dynamic approach. *Psychological Review, 94,* 84–106.

Seuren, P. A. M. (1985). *Discourse semantics.* Oxford: Basil Blackwell.

Shattuck-Hufnagel, S. (1979). Speech errors as evidence for a serial-ordering mechanism in sentence production. In W. E. Cooper & E. C. T. Walker (Eds) *Sentence processing: Psycholinguistic studies presented to Merrill Garrett* (pp. 295–342). Hillsdale, NJ: Lawrence Erlbaum.

Sperber, D., & Wilson, D. (1986). *Relevance: Communication and cognition.* Oxford: Basil Blackwell.

Sternberg, S., Wright, C. E., Knoll, R. L., & Monsell, S. (1980). Motor programs in rapid speech: Additional evidence. In R. A. Cole (Ed.) *Perception and production of fluent speech* (pp. 507–534). Hillsdale, NJ: Lawrence Erlbaum.

Stevens, K. N., & Blumstein, S. E. (1981). The search for invariant acoustic correlates of phonetic features. In P. D. Eimas & J. L. Miller (Eds) *Perspectives on the study of speech* (pp. 1–38). Hillsdale, NJ: Lawrence Erlbaum.

Tyler, L., & Warren, P. (1987). Local and global structure in spoken language comprehension. *Journal of Memory and Language, 26,* 638–657.

Wundt, W. (1900). *Die Sprache* (2 vols). Leipzig: Kröner.

Zwitserlood, P. (1989). The effects of sentential-semantic context in spoken-word processing. *Cognition, 32,* 25–64.

4

THINKING AND REASONING

Jonathan St B. T. Evans
University of Plymouth, Plymouth, England

The nature of human thought and the capacity for rational reasoning have been issues of great interest to philosophers and psychologists since the time of Aristotle. Humans have excelled among species in their ability to solve problems and to adapt their environment for their own purposes. We are unique in our possession of a highly sophisticated system of language allowing both representation of complex and abstract concepts and the communication of very precise meaning with one another. We have also developed a new form of evolution — much faster than natural selection — whereby the accumulated knowledge and wisdom of our culture is recorded and passed on through education so that each new generation starts with an advantage on the one before. Despite this impressive record, we also are subject to many systematic errors and biases in our thinking, some of which are discussed in this chapter.

The study of thinking and reasoning in humans can accurately be described as the study of the nature of intelligence. The work described here falls, however, into a quite different tradition from the psychometric study of individual differences in intelligent performance that is usually referred to as the psychology of intelligence. Psychometrics is concerned with the measurement of intelligent performance, whereas the study of thinking and reasoning is focused on understanding the nature of intelligent processes. Strangely enough, these turn out to be two quite different kinds of undertaking.

THE NATURE OF THINKING: AN HISTORICAL PERSPECTIVE

Historically, we can trace three different conceptions of the nature of thinking. The first of these corresponds to what the non-psychologist might respond if asked to define thought. I shall describe this notion as the *contents of consciousness*. Common sense (or *folk* psychology) supposes that we are consciously in control of our actions: we think, therefore we do. When we make a decision or solve a problem it is on the basis of a train of thought of which we are conscious and which we can, if required, describe to another. Such reports of thought are known as *introspections*. The validity of introspection is clearly assumed in our everyday folk psychology, as we all feel able to ask and answer questions about how and why we have taken particular actions. Indeed, a major industry – opinion polling – is based upon introspectionism. Politicians and political commentators alike are absorbed by the results of polls that ask people not only how they intend to vote, but also to identify the issues which will influence their decisions.

Aristotle and other early philosophers were in no doubt that the mind could and should study itself through introspection. This led to a theory of thinking known as *associationism* in which thinking was supposed to consist of a sequence of images linked by one of several principles (see Mandler & Mandler, 1964). Associationism and the equation of thought with consciousness remained more or less unchallenged until the late nineteenth and early twentieth centuries when several separate developments conspired to challenge this idea.

First, there were the systematic experimental studies of introspection carried out at the Würzburg School around the beginning of the twentieth century (see Humphrey, 1951). In these experiments, subjects were asked to perform simple cognitive acts such as giving word associations or judging the comparative weight of two objects and then asked to report on what went through their minds at the time. Much to the initial surprise of the researchers, many of these acts did not appear to be mediated by conscious thoughts. Subjects often reported either no conscious experience at all, or else one of indescribable or "imageless" thought.

A second influential development was that of the Freudian school of psychoanalysis which introduced the notion of unconscious thought and motivation. An introspective report of the reason for an action would certainly be suspect to a Freudian since it might well constitute a *rationalization* of behaviour determined by deep-seated and repressed emotions in the unconscious mind.

The other major influence was the introduction of the school of behaviourism by J. B. Watson (e.g., 1920) whose influence was very strong in psychology up until the 1950s and which lingers on even in the present day. Watson attacked all study of conscious thought as mentalistic and unscientific. Science, he maintained, could concern itself only with the study of phenomena that were subject to objective observation and independent verification – criteria that introspective reports clearly could not meet. Watson and other behaviourists effectively redefined thought as simply complex forms of behaviour which were the result of stimulus–response learning. Study of stimulus–response pairings and reinforcement history were sufficient to explain all phenomena attributed – by the mentalistically inclined – to thinking.

From the viewpoint of a modern cognitive psychologist both introspectionists and behaviourists might be seen as half right. The behaviourists were probably right in their contention that thought cannot be studied effectively via introspection. The mentalists, on the other hand, were correct in asserting that complex behaviour could not be explained without reference to internal mental processes. Their mistake – with the benefit of hindsight – was to assume that such processes were necessarily conscious and reportable. This leads us to the third conception of human thought – that of *information processing*.

Psychologists' own thinking – like that of their subjects – is constrained by the availability of models and analogies. Watson used the analogy of a telephone exchange to explain his notion of learning by stimulus–response connections. Although its origin can be traced to earlier, highly creative thinkers (especially Craik, 1943) the emergence of cognitive psychology in the 1950s and 1960s was largely due to the development of cybernetic systems and then the digital computer. Computers are general-purpose information processing systems. They compute by manipulating symbols which can represent almost anything – numbers and arithmetical operators, permitting arithmetic; letters and words as in word and text processing; collections of facts stored in a database; and so on.

When people perform mental arithmetic, we would describe this as an act of thought. So is a computer also thinking when it performs computations to solve problems? It appears that it is, although some philosophers (e.g., Searle, 1980) maintain that computer intelligence is intrinsically different from that of the human mind. The point of the analogy, however, is that we can see that computers can perform complex acts of information processing – depending upon their programming – but without any need to assume that they are conscious. Once you equate thinking with information processing, then the task of the modern cognitive psychologist is clear: understanding thought is the problem of discovering the software of the human brain. Many psychological theories in fact are formulated as working computer programs which attempt to simulate the behaviour of a human being who is solving a problem or engaged in some other cognitive activity.

In spite of this advance, arguments persist among cognitive and social psychologists as to the value of introspective reports. Some cognitive psychologists disregard them entirely on the basis of much evidence that such reports can be both incomplete and misleading (Nisbett & Wilson, 1977). One interesting line of argument is that verbal reports *are* useful indicators of thought processes but not as used in the tradition of introspective reporting (Ericsson & Simon, 1980). According to this view, verbalizations are the *products* of cognitive processes and can be fruitfully interpreted by the psychologist when subjects are asked to "think aloud" while performing a task or solving a problem. Introspective reports fail because first, they are retrospective rather than concurrent, and second, they invite subjects to describe their thinking or to theorize about the causes of their behaviour.

The psychology of thinking can be broadly defined to cover a wide range of topics. For example, Gilhooly (1982) distinguishes between *directed thinking* — as found in problem solving and reasoning — *undirected thinking* — as in day-dreaming — and *creative thinking*. In this chapter we shall focus on directed thinking: thought aimed at achieving specific goals. This is an area in which reasonable theoretical progress has been made, and for which there are clear practical applications in everyday life.

Studies of directed thinking fall broadly into three main areas which are described as problem solving, reasoning, and decision-making. We shall consider each in turn.

PROBLEM SOLVING

A person has a problem whenever he or she wishes to achieve a goal and is unable to proceed immediately to do so. Problem solving consists of finding a method of getting from where you are to where you want to be, using such resources and knowledge as you have available. This definition obviously covers a vast range of human activity; problem solving is clearly involved in solving crossword puzzles and choosing chess moves, but it is equally involved in finding your way to a new destination, obtaining a ticket for a sold-out sporting contest, or working out how to persuade your boss to give you a pay rise.

One distinction which has helped psychologists think about the vast range of behaviours involved in problem solving is that between well-defined and ill-defined problems. In a well-defined problem, all the information needed and the means of solution are available at the outset. This is typical of things that are set as "problems" in newspapers, and so on, and also typical of much research in the psychological laboratory. An anagram is an example of a well-defined problem. You know the letters that constitute the solution word and also the means of solving the problem — rearrangement of the order of letters — at the outset. Well-defined problem solving thus consists of applying known rules to known information in order to transform the situation and achieve the goal.

61

Some of the most famous studies of well-defined problem solving were conducted by Newell and Simon (1972). An example of one of their problems is cryptarithmetic, in which subjects were given the following problem:

DONALD
+ GERALD

= ROBERT

Subjects are also told that D = 5 and that each letter represents a single digit number between 0 and 9. Given this information and the assumption that the normal rules of arithmetic apply, it is possible – though complicated – to work out what all the letter–number pairings must be. If the reader wishes to attempt this problem, then it is suggested that a good record (on paper) of the sequence of attempts – including errors and correction – be kept.

Newell and Simon (1972) made an important theoretical contribution with the idea of problem solving as a search through a *problem space*. A problem space consists of a number of linked *states* including an initial or starting state and one or more goal states. All problems include *permissible operators* which allows one state to be transformed to another. Thus, solving problem consists in applying operators repeatedly to transform the initial state into a goal state.

As an example consider the game of chess (also studied by Newell & Simon, 1972). The states of the game can be described as the position of the pieces on the board plus some additional information (whose turn is it to move, do players have the right to castle, may a pawn be captured *en passant*, and so on). The initial state is thus the board with the pieces in starting position with White having the right to move. A goal state is any position in which the player has won the game either by checkmating the opponent or making such a mate inevitable. The permissible operators are the laws of chess, which determine the moves that can legally be made in a given situation.

Note that these definitions tell us nothing about the strategy of chess. The problem space consists of all states that can be reached by legal moves – a vast number of possibilities in the case of chess. The strategy of the game obviously consists in choosing between alternative legal moves in such a way as to move towards the goal state of a winning position. In chess, as in many other problems, the problem space is too large for an exhaustive search to be feasible. You cannot consider all moves and all possible replies to more than a very few moves ahead without the number of possible positions becoming enormous. Thus Newell and Simon (1972) emphasize the importance of *heuristic* strategies. An heuristic is a short-cut, rule of thumb method which may lead to a quick solution, but which may also fail. What heuristics do is to drastically reduce the size of the problem space to be searched in the hope that the goal state is not excluded in the process.

Consider the following anagram: GBANRIEK. Since it has eight letters the total problem space includes the 8! = 40,320 possible rearrangements of the letters. A guaranteed, *algorithmic* (i.e., exhaustive search) method of solving this involves constructing all 40,320 letter strings and checking whether each is a word. A typical heuristic method, on the other hand, might involve looking for familiar letter patterns to decompose the problem. For example, we note that the anagram includes the letters I, N, and G and speculate that the word might be of the form _____ING. Thus we have now reduced the problem to solving the five-letter anagram BAREK which has only 5! (120) possible solutions and is thus much easier. We may now spot the solution word BREAKING. Like all heuristics, however, this was not guaranteed to work. Many words contain the letters ING in other configurations, e.g., GELATIN.

Problem space analysis is extremely useful as it provides a common framework in which to describe a very wide range of different problems. Newell and Simon (1972) studied subjects using think-aloud protocols while solving problems such as the cryptarithmetic example given above. They concluded that people have sets of general-purpose problem solving strategies that are used in similar ways to search problem spaces, no matter what particular domain is involved. They implemented their theory in a working computer program called General Problem Solver that was claimed to solve the same problems as the human subjects and in a similar way.

Important though this work has been, the conclusions are somewhat questionable. The first difficulty is that most real-life problems are ill defined. Some aspect of the problem – the information assumed, the means of solution, sometimes even the goal – is incomplete or missing at the outset. Take the case of engineering design which was subjected to detailed psychological study by Ball, Evans and Dennis (in press). An engineer is given a general specification for a device which includes its functionality – what it must do – and a number of constraints, including costs. The engineer must then come up with a technical specification for a device which can be constructed and can be demonstrated to work.

As Ball discovered, such problems are not at all well defined. Nearly all the information required to solve the problem is implicit and must be retrieved either from the existing knowledge and experience of the engineer or by researching technical manuals, and so on. In the process of design, constraints emerge that were not apparent at the outset. The goal initially set may also be modified and rethought as the work progresses. Now such activity can still be usefully described within the problem space framework – a space that is being continually augmented and redefined by the knowledge and experience of the engineer. However, the point is that simply applying the problem space description provides no explanation for some of the most important aspects of the process, particularly the means by which prior knowledge and experience are retrieved and applied.

A number of more recent studies of human problem solving have focused on ill-defined problems and the use of prior knowledge. Of particular interest has been the role of analogy in solving problems (see Gick & Holyoak, 1980, 1983; Keane, 1988). Most real-life problem solving – including "expert" problem solving – occurs within contexts where the solver has previous experience. Clearly, people do not solve all such problems as if seen for the first time; they must extrapolate from past experience. The theoretical and practical interest lies in how they actually bring their prior knowledge to bear.

A problem that has featured in many of these studies is the *tumour problem* first introduced by the Gestalt psychologist Duncker (1945). The problem is that of a patient who has a malignant but inoperable tumour that can be destroyed only by radiation. However, the radiation destroys healthy tissue at the same rate as diseased tissue. The solution that subjects must find is to use a lens to converge the rays at the point of the tumour. Hence, the rays accumulate only to sufficient intensity to destroy the tumour and not the healthy tissue they pass through on the way (see Figure 1).

The problem is incompletely defined in that while the goal and constraints are generally indicated, subjects must search their knowledge and imagination for possible means of solution. General knowledge of medical procedures is unhelpful; surgery is out by definition; drug treatments are of no relevance. The problem can, however, be facilitated by provision of a structural analogue such as the General story. The General is trying to attack a fortress which is well defended and which may be reached by a number of different roads. Each road is mined and may be safely crossed only by a small band of men. The General splits his force into small groups which approach

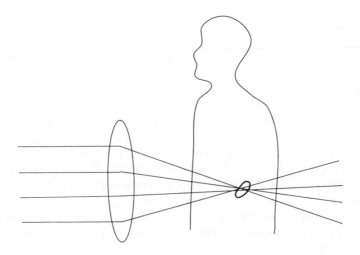

Figure 1   Solution to Duncker's tumour problem

simultaneously from different directions, and converge at the fortress with sufficient force to win the battle.

Gick and Holyoak (1980) showed that presentation of the General story could facilitate convergence solutions to the tumour problem provided that subjects were given a cue as to its relevance. There is a theoretical argument as to whether analogies can work by direct mapping of the elements of the analogy on to the problem, or whether the solution is mediated by an abstract *schema*. Gick and Holyoak suggest that subjects may construct and apply a *convergence schema* which is defined in terms of variables. For example, in the schema the goal is to destroy an obstacle, the means is a sufficient force, the constraint is that direct application is blocked, and so on. The General story could lead to development of a schema which is applied to the tumour problem.

The notion of schema is a useful one, in that it helps us to understand how knowledge may be abstracted, generalized, and applied in new situations. The notion will recur in the discussion of reasoning to which we now turn.

REASONING

Reasoning is the process of drawing conclusions or inferences from given information. An important distinction is that between deductive and inductive inference. Deductive reasoning involves drawing conclusions that are logically valid, that is, they necessarily follow from the premises on which they are based. Thus such inferences do not increase the amount of information contained in the premises; they merely render explicit what was previously latent information. The following are examples of valid deductive inferences:

> The television will work only if it is plugged into the mains;
> The television is not plugged into the mains,
> Therefore, the television will not work.
>
> John is taller than Jim;
> Paul is shorter than Jim,
> Therefore, John is taller than Paul.

The validity of the first example does not depend in any way on our knowledge of television sets, but only on our understanding of the connective "only if". Any argument of the form *p only if q; not-q, therefore not-p* would be logically valid no matter what propositions we substitute for *p* and *q*. Hence, validity depends on the form of the argument, not its actual content. In logic, the statement *p only if q* cannot be true in a world where *p* is the case and *q* is not the case. Hence, once we know that *q* is false we can infer that *p* must be false as well.

The second example requires us to know that the relation taller–shorter is *transitive*. A transitive relation is one where the objects are ordered in a single line so that whenever A is higher than B on the scale, and B is above C then A is also above C. Examples of other transitive relations are better–worse, warmer–colder, and darker–lighter. Many relations, of course, are not transitive. If A is next to B and B is next to C it does not follow that A is next to C.

Deductive inferences are very important in intelligent thinking as they allow knowledge to be stored in generalities and then applied to particular situations. Thus if we want to watch television and discover one that is unplugged, we immediately plug it in. This is a simple example of reasoning in order to solve a problem. The limitation of deductive reasoning, however, is that it adds no new knowledge; thus we cannot learn by deduction. Induction is involved whenever our conclusion has more information than the premises. A typical example is an inductive generalization such as

> The Australian soap operas I have seen were boring, hence all Australian soap operas are boring.

Such an inference is clearly not logically valid, though it could well influence what you watch when you get the TV plugged in.

The British psychologist, Peter Wason, invented two famous problems that have been used extensively to study both inductive and deductive reasoning. The inductive problem was first published by Wason (1960) and is known as the "2 4 6" task. The subjects are told that the experimenter has a rule in mind which applies to "triples" of three whole numbers. An example which conforms to the rule is "2 4 6". The subjects are then asked to discover the rule by generating triples of their own. In each case the experimenter says whether the triple conforms or not. Subjects are told to announce the rule only when they are very sure that they know it.

The actual rule is "any ascending sequence" but the subject is induced by the example to form a more specific hypothesis, such as "ascending with equal intervals". Most subjects have great difficulty in solving the problem initially because all the examples they test appear to conform to the rule. The reason is that subjects test positive examples of their hypothesis which invariably turn out to be positive examples of the experimenter's rule as well. Their hypothesis can be refuted only by testing a negative example of the hypothesis such as "1 2 4" which is revealed as a positive instance of the actual rule. The set relationships involved are shown in Figure 2.

The protocols discussed by Wason (1960) were very interesting, suggesting that some subjects became so convinced of the correctness of their hypotheses that they were led to reformulate the proposed rule in different terms when told it was wrong. A striking example of this is shown in Table 1.

Wason's interpretation of his findings was that subjects have a confirmation bias, meaning that they systematically seek out evidence that confirms rather than refutes their current hypothesis. He suggested that such a confirmation bias is a very general tendency in human thought which may

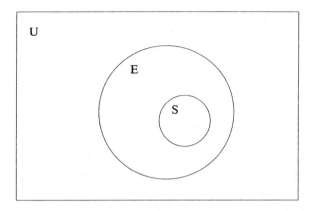

U   Universal set of all triples
E   Experimenter's rule – all
    triples in ascending sequence
S   Subjects' hypothesis, e.g.,
    ascending with equal intervals

Figure 2   Set relationships in Wason's 2 4 6 task

Table 1   Example protocol from Wason (1960)

8 10 12: two added each time; 14 16 18: even numbers in order or magnitude;
20 22 24: same reason; 1 3 5: two added to preceding number.

The rule is that by starting with any number two is added each time to form the next number.

2 6 10: middle number is arithmetic mean of other two; 1 50 99: same reason

The rule is that the middle number is the arithmetic mean of the outer two.

3 10 17: same number, seven, added each time; 0 3 6: three added each time.

The rule is that the difference between two numbers next to each other is the same.

12 8 4: the same number subtracted each time to form the next number.

The rule is adding a number, always the same one, to form the next number.

1 4 9: any three numbers in order of magnitude.

The rule is any three numbers in order of magnitude.

(17 minutes)

account for the maintenance of prejudice and false belief. While a number of authors have accepted this interpretation, it has also been subject to serious challenge (see Evans, 1989; Klayman & Ha, 1987).

The problem is that the subjects in the "2 4 6" experiment have no way of knowing that a positive test cannot lead to refutation of their hypothesis, and in many real-world situations it would do so. For example, in science it is customary to formulate general hypotheses and test if they apply to specific cases. Hence, given the hypothesis "All metals expand when heated" you would test any untried metal to see if the prediction holds — and if it did not you would indeed refute the hypothesis. You would not be likely to try heating non-metal things, and even if you did and they expanded, it would mean only that your rule was insufficiently general.

Arguments such as these have led some authors to suggest that subjects' behaviour on the "2 4 6" is more rational than it at first appears and that if there is a bias, it is towards positive testing rather than to confirmation as such. A particularly interesting experiment reported by Tweney, Doherty, and Mynatt (1980) provides evidence for this. In one study, instead of defining instances in positive and negative terms (right/wrong, belonging/not-belonging) they told subjects that all triples were either MEDs or DAXes and that "2 4 6" was an example of a MED. What happened was that subjects continued to test their hypotheses positively but alternated between testing MED and DAX hypotheses. For example, if the hypothesis was that "triples ascending in equal intervals are MEDs and others are DAXes", then they might test "1 2 5" predicting it to be a DAX. This meant that they effectively tested negative examples of the usual hypothesis and hence solved the problem much more easily. The psychological difference is that the negative test of MED was construed as a positive test of DAX.

A close parallel to these findings occurs with the second and most famous of Wason's problems — the four-card selection task (see Evans, Newstead and Byrne 1993 for detailed review and discussion). This problem requires subjects to test hypotheses via deductive reasoning. In the classic "abstract" version of the task, subjects are told that a set of cards always has a capital letter on one side and a single-figure number on the the other side. They are then shown four such cards lying on a table with the exposed values as shown in Figure 3. The subjects are told that the following rule may be true or false:

If there is an A on one side of the card then there is a 3 on the other side of the card.

The subjects' task is to turn over those cards — and only those cards — that are needed to decide whether the rule is true or false. The task is deceptively simple, since most subjects fail to solve it. The common answers given are A alone, or A and 3. The correct answer is the A and the 7. The reason is that the rule can be shown to be false only if there is an A on one side of a card and number other than a 3 on the other. Only by turning the A and the 7 (not a 3) is it possible to discover such a card. There is also no point

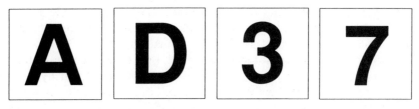

Figure 3   The four cards displayed in a version of Wason's selection task

in turning the 3 since the rule makes no claim that an A must be on the back of a 3.

Wason's original claim was again that card selections reflected a confirmation bias: subjects were trying to prove the rule true rather than false, that is, looking for the combination A and 3, rather than A and not-3. This view was, however, refuted to the satisfaction of Wason as well as other authors by the finding of "matching bias" reported by Evans and Lynch (1973). They pointed out that the preferred selections, A and 3, were not only the verifying choices, but also the positive choices matching the items named in the actual rule. Verification and matching could, however, be separated by introducing negative components into the rule. Consider for example, the rule

> *If there is an A on one side of the card then there is NOT a 3 on the other side of the card*

If subjects have a confirmation bias, then they should now choose the A and the 7 which confirm the two parts of the rule. If, however, they have a matching bias then they should continue to choose A and 3 which are the correct and *falsifying* combination on this rule. Subjects do, in fact, continue to choose predominantly matching values on this and other variants of the rule, thus confirming the predictions of Evans and Lynch. Evans (1989) regards matching as an example of a generalized *positivity bias*, that is, bias to think about positively defined items, which also accounts for subjects' behaviour on the "2 4 6" task.

Dozens of experiments have been published – and continue to be published – in which subjects are asked to solve versions of the Wason selection task. Most of these have been concerned with the so-called thematic materials facilitation effect. This has its origin in two early studies discussed in Wason and Johnson-Laird's (1972) famous textbook on reasoning. In one of these (Johnson-Laird, Legrenzi, & Legrenzi, 1972) subjects were shown envelopes in place of cards, together with the following Postal Rule:

> *If the letter is sealed then it has a 50 lire stamp on it.*

Subjects were then shown four envelopes which were either front side up and showing a 50 or 40 lire stamp, or rear side up showing that they were sealed or unsealed (see Figure 4). The subjects had to decide which envelopes to turn

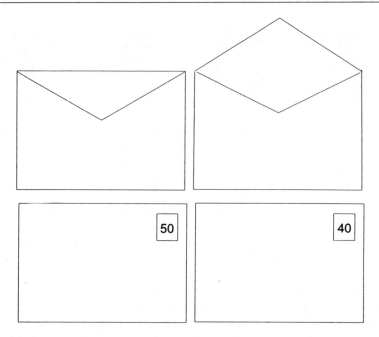

Figure 4 The four envelopes shown to subjects in the Postal Rule version of the selection task

over in order to decide if the rule was true or false. The usual matching response on the abstract task would lead to choice of the sealed envelope and the 50 lire stamp. However, almost all subjects made the logically correct choice of the sealed envelope and the one showing a 40 lire stamp.

The original interpretation offered of this and other similar experiments was that use of thematic materials facilitated logical reasoning on the task. This view has been considerably refined by subsequent research, however. The problem with the Postal Rule is that a very similar rule (involving pence rather than lire) was in force in the UK at the time of the study. Thus it was argued that subjects knew from experience that envelopes with a lower value stamp must not be sealed and that hence no "reasoning" as such was required to solve the problem. This argument was supported by the findings of several later studies which showed that first, the Postal Rule produces no facilitation of performance in American subjects unfamiliar with such a rule, and second, British subjects too young to remember the rule (it was dropped in the 1970s) show no facilitation on the problem whereas older subjects perform much better.

It is not the case, however, that subjects must have direct experience of the context in order for a problem content to facilitate on the selection task. A very effective version, for example, is the Sears Problem in which subjects are asked to play the role of a store manager checking that a company rule has been followed. The rule is

If a purchase exceeds $30, then the receipt must be approved by the departmental manager.

Subjects are shown four receipts, two of which are front side up showing totals of above and below $30 and two of which are front side down and either have or do not have the signature of the departmental manager on them. Few subjects have any difficulty in correctly deciding to turn over the receipt for more than $30, and the one that has *not* been signed by the manager. This is despite the fact that subjects have not worked as managers in department stores.

While arguments exist about the precise reason for facilitation of performance by these kinds of thematic content, the general idea is that where subjects have either direct or analogous experience that can be linked to the problem, then they can solve it. Another line of argument is that it is the introduction of deontic terms such as *may* and *must* which carry with them notions of permission and obligation that causes the facilitation. The idea is that we have generalized reasoning schemas that enable us to understand the logic of any situation in which, for example, a precondition is set for an action. Thus, once we have identified the action (e.g., sealing an envelope, spending over $30) and the precondition (sufficient value stamp, permission of departmental manager) we know what to do: we are applying a generalized permission schema to the problem at hand.

The two problems of Peter Wason discussed in this section have stimulated much interesting psychological work on the nature of human reasoning. The specific findings discussed here invite two general conclusions: first, that reasoning with "abstract" problem material is heavily biased by a tendency to think about positively rather than negatively defined information, and second, that the introduction of thematic problem content, and hence associated prior knowledge, can have a dramatic effect on the reasoning observed, and sometimes produces much better logical performance. The "sometimes" in the latter conclusion is needed. Other research, which there is no space to discuss here, has also indicated that prior knowledge can be a source of bias and error in reasoning. This is especially the case when subjects are asked to evaluate the logic of an argument but have strong prior beliefs about the truth of a conclusion (see Evans, 1989, chap. 4).

DECISION MAKING AND STATISTICAL JUDGEMENT

In a problem solving task, it is normally possible to work out and demonstrate a solution to the problem set. Once you have the solution, you know it and can prove it. In a decision-making task, however, subjects are required to exercise judgement about a choice that will only later prove to work out well or badly. Decision-making means committing yourself to choices between actions by anticipation of what the outcomes will – or may – be. Thus when we make any decision – to accept one job rather than another, to marry someone or not, go to a football match rather than stay at home – we do so in the hope that the future we chose was to be preferred to the one we avoided.

Decision-making is obviously of great importance in the real world, but it is a subject of considerable psychological interest too. Most real-world decision-making is done under conditions of uncertainty: we do not know for sure what will happen as a result of each choice and at best can try to estimate the probabilities of different outcomes. If we are to choose rationally then we need to evaluate the desirability of these outcomes as well. In the parlance of decision theory, we should try to maximize *expected utility* where utility is the subjective value of the outcome and where the term "expectation" means that we weight the various possible outcomes by their likelihood of occurring. Hence, a small chance of a highly desirable outcome might be equally attractive to a much better prospect of a less desirable outcome.

There has been much debate in the psychological literature about whether people choose rationally or not. The notion of rational choice has several components. First, it implies that people will consciously consider the various actions available to them and try to project ahead the possible outcomes and further choices to which they lead in what is termed a *decision tree*. Second, it is assumed that they assign probabilities and utilities to each of these outcomes as accurately as possible in the light of their current beliefs. Finally, rational decision-makers are assumed to apply systematic principles, such as the maximization of expected utility, in order to decide their final choices.

There are many demonstrations of human choice behaviour that appear to depart from this idealized notion. Within the space restriction here I shall discuss just one aspect – the ability of people to judge probabilities or to reason statistically. A famous set of papers by the psychologists Amos Tversky and Daniel Kahneman dating from the early 1970s have apparently demonstrated the frailty of human probability judgement. This research is often cited as evidence of irrationality, although Tversky and Kahneman themselves follow the tradition of work on "bounded rationality" espoused by Newell and Simon (1972). The idea is that people cannot base their probability judgements on probability theory due its computational complexity and instead employ short-cut rules of thumb known as *heuristics*. While often useful, such heuristics can also lead to systematic errors and biases.

Of the heuristics discussed by Kahneman and Tversky, the two most famous are those of *representativeness* and *availability* (see Kahneman, Slovic, & Tversky, 1982 for a collection of relevant papers, including the seminal ones). Probability or frequency of an event is estimated by the availability heuristic when people base their judgement on the ease with which examples can be brought to mind. Such a heuristic would often be effective.

For example, an experienced doctor might base a provisional diagnosis on her recollection of the numbers of previous cases or patients with similar symptoms who turned out to suffer from a particular condition. Assuming that memory was accurate and that experience was representative then this is a good, if rough basis for a judgement.

As Tversky and Kahneman have demonstrated, however, relying on availability of recalled examples can lead to biases. For example, some types of information are easier to retrieve than others, due to the way in which memory is organized. For example, most people will say, if asked, that there are more words in English that start with the letter k than those that have k as the third letter, although the reverse is true. The problem is that it is hard to generate examples of the latter category: they cannot easily be "brought to mind".

Availability is also implicated in biases which preserve false beliefs and theories. An interesting example is the phenomenon of *illusory correlation*. It has been demonstrated in a number of studies that human judges — including experts — hold theories that are not supported by the evidence they encounter. For example, some clinicians maintain that projective personality tests such as the Rorschach ink blot test is useful in diagnosing mental illness despite a lack of any supporting evidence. Research has shown that such judges perceive a correlation between test results and diagnoses in a set of data in which they are in fact randomly related. A plausible explanation of illusory correlation is that the judges selectively remember the cases that confirm their expectations or pet theories. Thus confirming cases are more available in later recall and bias the judgement of the correlation.

The representativeness heuristic is involved in judgements of conditional probability. The likelihood of a sample given a population, or of an event given a hypothesis is dependent upon the perceived similarity of the two. Similarity judgements may, however, cause the subject to overlook the relevance of a critical statistical feature such as the size of the sample, or the base rate occurrence of the event. A simple example is provided by the conjunction fallacy (Tversky & Kahneman, 1983). Subjects are given a description of Bill as follows:

Bill is [brief description of Bill]

They are then asked to rank the likelihood of several statements including the following:

a Bill is an accountant
b Bill plays jazz for a hobby
c Bill is an accountant who plays jazz for a hobby.

What happens is that most subjects rate the order of likelihood of these statements as $a > c > b$. However, there is a statistical impossibility here in that statement c cannot be more likely than statement b. Given two events A and

B the probability of them both occurring – $P(A \cap B)$ – must be less than or equal to the probability of either $P(A)$ or $P(B)$. Whenever c is true then b is true as well, because Bill plays jazz for a hobby. If all jazz players were accountants then the two statements would be equally likely, otherwise b has to be more probable.

The explanation offered for the fallacy is that the description of Bill conforms to our stereotype for accountants but not for jazz players. Thus the statement c is more representative of the description than is statement b and hence judged more probable.

One of the most famous of Kahneman and Tversky's problems is the Cabs Problem. You are given the following information: in a certain city there are two cab companies: the Blue cab company, which has 85 per cent of the city's cabs, and the Green cab company, which has 15 per cent of the city's cabs. A cab is involved in a hit-and-run accident and a witness later identified the cab as a Green one. Under tests the witness was shown to be able to identify the colour of a cab correctly about 80 per cent of the time under comparable viewing conditions. The subjects are asked if the cab involved in the accident is more likely to have been Green or Blue. Most say Green, although the correct answer is Blue.

The problem is that subjects disregard the base rate or prior probability of the cab colour – 85 : 15 in favour of Blue. In fact, when asked to give a numerical estimate, most subjects say 80 per cent Green – the chance of the witness correctly identifying a cab. If there were no witnesses, it would be obvious that the chance of the cab being Blue was 85 per cent – the base rate. As Figure 5 shows, however, the chance of a Blue cab being identified as Green is 17 per cent which is still higher than the chance (12 per cent) of a Green cab being identified as Green.

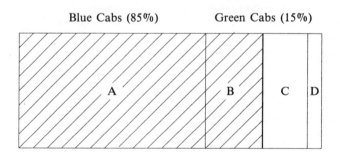

Blue Cabs (85%)   Green Cabs (15%)

A	B	C	D

A   Probability of Blue identified as Blue $= 80\% \times 85\% = 68\%$
B   Probability of Blue identified as Green $= 20\% \times 85\% = 17\%$
C   Probability of Green identified as Green $= 80\% \times 15\% = 12\%$
D   Probability of Green identified as Blue $= 20\% \times 15\% = 3\%$

Figure 5 Probabilities in the Cabs Problem

Originally, the base rate fallacy was interpreted as the base rate lacking representativeness, although the explanation is probably more fundamental. We find it very difficult to apply abstract statistics to individual cases. Hence, many cigarette smokers are aware of the statistical risks for smokers as a whole, but do not feel that this affects them as individuals. However, we can apply statistics when we see a causal connection. If the cabs problem is slightly reworded, most subjects give the right answer. In this version the number of Green and Blue cabs in the city is the same, but 85 per cent of the cabs *involved in accidents* are Blue. The image of reckless Blue cab drivers conjured up induces subjects to take account of the base rate, although from a statistical point of view the problem is unchanged.

CONCLUSIONS

Psychological research on thinking and reasoning has produced some useful – and sometimes surprising – conclusions. The common-sense view, that intelligent actions are based on conscious and rational acts of thinking, does not fit the evidence at all well. If thought is to be defined as the information processing that underlies problem solving, reasoning, and decision-making, then surprisingly little of this appears to be accessible through introspection.

If human thinking is rational – and the success of the species suggests that it should be – then that rationality is highly constrained by our capacity to process information. In particular, we seem to solve problems and make decisions largely on the basis of heuristic processes which serve us well in some circumstances, but lead us into error and bias in others. We seem to have particular difficulty in understanding probability and uncertainty despite the crucial role that this plays in rational decision-making.

Studies of reasoning also show that we are prone to biases, for example in a strong preference for thinking about positively defined information. Perhaps the most important finding in this area, however, is the discovery that we do not – as was once thought – appear to reason by the use of an abstract mental logic, but instead seem to be highly influenced by the content and context of the problems with which we are faced. The processes of human thought appear to be quite specific to the areas of knowledge which we are involved in applying.

FURTHER READING

Baron, J. (1988). *Thinking and deciding*. Cambridge: Cambridge University Press.

Evans, J. St B. T. (1989). *Bias in human reasoning: Causes and consequences*. Hove: Lawrence Erlbaum.

Johnson-Laird, P. N., & Byrne, R. M. J. (1991). *Deduction*. Hove: Lawrence Erlbaum.

Kahney, H. (1987). *Problem solving: A cognitive approach*. Milton Keynes: Open University Press.

Von Winderfeldt, D., & Edwards, W. (1986). *Decision analysis and human behavioural research*. Cambridge: Cambridge University Press.

REFERENCES

Ball, L. J., Evans, J. St B. T. and Dennis (in press). *Cognitive processes in engineering design: a longitudinal study (Ergonomics)*. Unpublished PhD thesis, Polytechnic South West.

Craik, K. J. W. (1943). *The nature of explanation*. Cambridge: Cambridge University Press.

Duncker, K. (1945). On problem solving. *Psychological Monographs*, *58*, whole no. 270.

Ericsson, K. A., & Simon, H. A. (1980). Verbal reports as data. *Psychological Review*, *87*, 215–251.

Evans, J. St B. T. (1989). *Bias in human reasoning: Causes and consequences*. Hove and London: Lawrence Erlbaum.

Evans, J. St B. T., & Lynch, J. S. (1973). Matching bias in the selection task. *British Journal of Psychology*, *64*, 391–397.

Evans, J. St B. T., Newstead, S. E. and Byrne R. M. J. (1993). *Human reasoning*: *The psychology of deduction*. Hove and London: Lawrence Erlbaum.

Gick, M. L., & Holyoak, K. J. (1980). Analogical problem solving. *Cognitive Psychology*, *12*, 306–355.

Gick, M. L., & Holyoak, K. J. (1983). Schema induction and analogical transfer. *Cognitive Psychology*, *15*, 1–38.

Gilhooly, K. J. G. (1982). *Thinking: Directed, undirected and creative*. London: Academic Press.

Humphrey, C. (1951). *Thinking: An introduction to its experimental psychology*. London: Methuen.

Johnson-Laird, P. N., Legrenzi, P., & Legrenzi, M. S. (1972). Reasoning and a sense of reality. *British Journal of Psychology*, *63*, 395–400.

Kahneman, D., Slovic, P., & Tversky, A. (1982). *Judgment under uncertainty: Heuristics and biases*. Cambridge: Cambridge University Press.

Keane, M. T. (1988). *Analogical problem solving*. Chichester: Horwood.

Klayman, J., & Ha, Y.-W. (1987). Confirmation, disconfirmation and information in hypothesis testing. *Psychological Review*, *94*, 211–228.

Mandler, J. M., & Mandler, G. (1964). *Thinking: From association to Gestalt*. New York: Wiley.

Newell A., & Simon, H. A. (1972). *Human problem solving*. Englewood Cliffs, NJ: Prentice-Hall.

Nisbett, R. E., & Wilson, T. D. (1977). Telling more than we can know: Verbal reports on mental processes. *Psychological Review*, *84*, 231–295.

Nisbett, R. E., Fong, G. T., Lehman, D., & Cheng, P. W. (1987). Teaching reasoning. *Science*, *238*, 625–631.

Searle, J. R. (1980). Minds, brains and programs. *Behavioral and Brain Sciences*, *3*, 417–424.

Tversky, A., & Kahneman, D. (1983). Extensional vs intuitive reasoning: The conjunction fallacy in probability judgment. *Psychological Review*, *90*, 293–315.

Tweney, R. D., Doherty, M. E., & Mynatt, C. R. (1981). *On scientific thinking*. New York: Columbia University Press.

Wason, P. C. (1960). On the failure to eliminate hypotheses in a conceptual task. *Quarterly Journal of Experimental Psychology*, *12*, 129–140.

Wason, P. C. (1966). Reasoning. In B. M. Foss (Ed.) *New horizons in psychology I* (pp. 135–151). Harmondsworth: Penguin.

Wason, P. C., & Johnson-Laird, P. N. (1972). *Psychology of reasoning: Structure and content*. London: Batsford.

Watson, J. B. (1920). *Behaviorism*. New York: Norton.

5

ARTIFICIAL INTELLIGENCE

Alan Garnham
University of Sussex, England

Artificial intelligence, almost always known as AI, attempts to understand intelligent behaviour, in the broadest sense of that term, by getting computers to reproduce it. "Intelligent behaviour" is taken to include thinking, reasoning, and learning, and their prerequisites (perception, the mental representation of information, and the ability to use language). Indeed, much current work in AI is concerned with modelling aspects of behaviour that would not normally be thought of as requiring any special intelligence. As part of computer science, AI is separate from cognitive psychology, although there is a large overlap in subject area. The two come together (with, most importantly, linguistics and philosophy) in the multidisciplinary approach of cognitive science.

Although AI aims to understand human intelligence, it also aims to produce machines that behave intelligently, no matter what their underlying mechanism. However, although these machines may not model human behaviour, their construction may reflect principles that are useful in studying it.

HISTORY

Since AI depends on computers, it is a relatively new discipline: the name was first used in the mid-1950s, though a few years earlier, pioneers such as Alan Turing in Britain and Claude Shannon in the United States had worked out how to write chess-playing computer programs. The dream of mechanized thought has, of course, a much longer history. The philosophers Blaise Pascal (1623–1662) and Gottfried Leibniz (1646–1716) built small calculating machines, and conceived grander schemes for formalizing thought processes. Charles Babbage (1792–1871) came nearer to building a universal computing machine, but was foiled by the limitations of having to use mechanical parts. Real computers had to wait for electronic components – first vacuum tubes, then semiconductors.

A conference at Dartford College, New Hampshire, in 1956 effectively launched AI research, even though its organizers felt disappointed at the time. In retrospect, the most important line of research discussed at the conference was that of Allen Newell and Herbert Simon (see e.g., Newell, Shaw, & Simon, 1957) on human problem solving. They proposed the idea of a *heuristic* ("rule-of-thumb") procedure for solving problems, and they shunned a line of research based on modelling the properties of networks of brain cells, which only assumed major importance again 25 years later, in the guise of connectionism. Newell and Simon's *information processing* approach was the dominant one in the early days of AI, and it remained influential throughout the 1960s – the so-called *semantic information processing* era. There was, however, a subtle shift of emphasis from a formal analysis of tasks to one based on the meaning of the information being processed. Furthermore, in attempting to tackle broader problems, such as natural language understanding, AI researchers quickly discovered that everyday tasks depend on huge amounts of background knowledge. To keep programs manageable, they were made to work in limited domains, in particular BLOCKSWORLD – a tabletop with prismatic blocks on it. It was hoped that programs that worked in these limited domains would *scale up* to real situations. In practice they did not, and in retrospect it is often obvious why they could not.

The 1970s was a somewhat disappointing period in "traditional" areas of AI research. Indeed, in the UK the Lighthill report (Lighthill, 1972) concluded that AI should not be a priority area for research. The late 1970s saw four important developments. The first was a shift in interest from specific computer programs to general principles. To some extent this development was linked to the second, the emergence of cognitive science, in which AI techniques are used with the primary goal of developing general theories of cognition, rather than with the more applied ("engineering") goal of building intelligent machines. The third development was a shift in the research topics seen as central to AI. In particular, fifteen years of research on the first *expert systems* was beginning to have spectacular payoffs (in the domains of mathematics, medical diagnosis, and determining the structure of complex organic molecules) and suddenly everyone wanted to write an expert system. In the short term, this enthusiasm generated additional funding and research, but it soon became apparent that an expert system in one domain could not necessarily be used as a model for one in another domain. If expert systems showed that real applications had to come to grips with formalizing real knowledge (as opposed to knowledge about toy domains), they also showed that this task was a formidable one. The fourth development was the re-emergence of neural network modelling, of the kind that had been largely set aside by those who espoused the Newell and Simon information processing approach. Theoretical developments together with the availability of larger, faster computers suddenly saw this approach producing important and enticing results.

The 1980s saw the working out of these developments. Although all remain important, all have faced disappointments. It is very hard to make an expert system that replaces an expert, though much easier to write a program that helps one. And it is hard to generalize the lessons learned in one domain of expertise. Cognitive science has not integrated its subdisciplines as closely as was hoped, and neural network modelling has still to show that it can make significant contributions to modelling abilities that call for complex information processing, in particular high-level processes in language understanding and thinking and reasoning.

KNOWLEDGE REPRESENTATION

Intelligent behaviour requires information to be stored, either in a short-term store or a long-term store or, more usually, both. One of the primary tasks of AI is therefore to produce an account of how information is represented in an intelligent system.

We know that the human nervous system has many parts, and that those parts probably operate in different ways. Nevertheless, there are many attractions in proposing that all information is stored in the same format. It may not be the form of information storage that differentiates information processing systems, but the nature of the information and the purpose for which it is used. Partly for this reason, many AI researchers have been attracted to the idea that information should be stored using the logical language known as *first order predicate calculus* (FOPC), and extensions of it that incorporate reasoning about time and modality. An additional attraction of this proposal is that, at least in principle, FOPC is computationally tractable: given a FOPC database, other facts implied by that database can be generated automatically. Other systems of representation are either not known to have or known not to have this property.

Unfortunately, although FOPC appears to have desirable properties, in practice it is extremely cumbersome to use. Partly because of the uniformity of the representation, facts in a large FOPC database can be difficult to find. Similarly, although there is a well-established procedure for drawing inferences from facts in a FOPC database (the resolution method, Robinson, 1965), it very quickly gets bogged down in making all but the simplest inferences. Furthermore, inferences made from a FOPC database cannot be overridden by new information. Everyday inferences can – they are said to be *non-monotonic*. For example, if I know that John is 25 years old and lives in Los Angeles, I infer that he can drive. If I subsequently learn that he suffers from epilepsy, I would probably withdraw my previous conclusion. Since the late 1970s there have been several attempts to construct non-monotonic logics, similar to FOPC but with additional rules of inference that violate monotonicity. There have also been attempts to formalize non-monotonic reasoning in other ways. The idea of a truth maintenance system (TMS) (Doyle, 1979) has been important in many of these. A TMS stores information about the justification for beliefs held, and allows *dependency-dependent backtracking*, so that when a belief turns out to be false, the reasons why it was held can be accessed directly and reassessed. None of these attempts to handle non-monotonic reasoning has been entirely successful.

Partly as a result of problems with uniform representation systems, such as FOPC, many AI researchers have proposed non-uniform representations, which allow special procedures for manipulating certain types of information. One of the earliest, and best-known, non-uniform representations is semantic networks (Quillian, 1968). Semantic networks give a special place to the information represented in their links and, in particular, they allow efficient processing of taxonomic information. Quillian's original, and rather simple, networks have been extended and elaborated in various ways, and representation of information in network form has proved a recurrent theme in AI. More complex non-uniform representation schemes that are related to semantic networks include frames and scripts. Scripts represent stereotyped sequences of events, frames have several uses. In one, frames represent particular objects and types of object, and a more recent development is that of object-oriented programming languages. The first widely used object-oriented language was the AI language SMALLTALK. More recently object-oriented versions of the most important AI language, LISP, have appeared, and languages such as C now have object-oriented versions (C++). Indeed, one of the major applications of object-oriented programming is not in AI, but in the development of windows-based interfaces for personal computers and workstations, where windows are treated as objects.

In the framework of semantic networks, the spread of activation through a network is the principal method of extracting information from it. This process has usually been simulated on a serial computer, but it ought to be achieved more efficiently on parallel hardware. Indeed, one of the most important parallel processing computers, the Connection Machine (not to be confused with connectionist neural nets), was inspired by Scott Fahlman's

(1979) suggestion for implementing semantic networks on special hardware. The idea of distributed processing is also found in neural network models of cognitive processing. Neural networks also allow, though they do not demand, distributed representations of the knowledge embodied in them. In particular, those neural networks that *learn* to perform tasks, rather than having information encoded into them by the programmer, are likely to develop distributed representations. Such networks show rule-governed behaviour as an emergent property, and the only way to determine exactly what rules such a network is following is to examine the relation between its inputs and its outputs.

There are many things we cannot be sure of, so a further issue in knowledge representation is the encoding and use of uncertain information. Inferences from uncertain information are modelled mathematically using probability theory and, in particular, Bayes' theorem, which is familiar to psychologists from statistical courses. Complex sets of probabilistic interrelations can be modelled in so-called *Bayesian networks*. Unfortunately Bayesian inference is neither computationally simple nor always the correct model of real world uncertain inference. The early expert system MYCIN (see below) introduced the simplifying idea of *certainty factors* associated with each of its diagnostic rules of inference. In recent years attention has focused on a more sophisticated mathematical approach known as Dempster-Shafer theory and there has also been renewed interest in fuzzy set theory, which enjoyed brief popularity in cognitive psychology in the mid-1970s.

VISION

Traditional AI research on vision was concerned, broadly speaking, with recognition of the objects – the prismatic solids – in the BLOCKSWORLD. For computer vision programs, the objects were matt white, uniformly lit (no shadows), and placed against a black background. In fact, the general problem of object recognition in the BLOCKSWORLD was set aside in favour of two of its component problems: finding lines in an image of a BLOCKSWORLD scene, and *segmenting* the image into sets of regions – each region corresponding to a surface – that belong to the same object. Indeed, this research came to be dominated by attempts to solve the segmentation problem: many programs required line drawings (rather than images) as their inputs.

The most important method of attempting to solve the segmentation problem, originally suggested by Alfonso Guzman (1968), was to use information about the types of vertex in the scene. Guzman's taxonomy was intuitive, but it was systematized independently by Max Clowes (1971) and David Huffman (1971), who stressed the importance of maintaining different descriptions of the image (in terms of lines, line junctions, and regions) and the scene (in terms of edges, vertices, and surfaces), and of making systematic inferences about the scene on the basis of the image. The Clowes-Huffman scheme is limited to scenes with no shadows and in which no more than three lines meet at any point. It has three types of line (corresponding to boundaries, inside edges, and outside edges) and four basic types of line junction (Ts, Ys, Ls, and arrows). From these line types and junction types, 16 *derived* junction types can be constructed, which correspond to possible

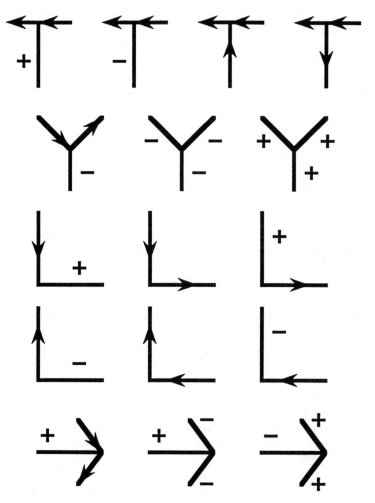

Figure 1 The 16 derived junction types in the Clowes-Huffman scheme – 4 Ts, 3 Ys, 6 Ls, and 3 arrows. An arrow on a line signifies that it represents an occluding edge (boundary between objects), a plus (+) sign signifies a convex (or outside) edge of a single object, and a minus (–) sign a concave (or inside) edge. The direction of the arrow indicates the side of the line on which the occluding object lies (to the right when facing in the direction of the arrow)

configurations in a BLOCKSWORLD scene (see Figure 1). Identification of the basic junction types in the image, plus the application of the constraint that any line should be of the same type along its whole length, allows most images of permissible scenes to be interpreted.

David Waltz (1975) extended the Clowes-Huffman scheme to scenes with shadows and to images in which more than three lines meet at a point. These apparently simple changes increased the number of permissible derived junction types from 16 to about 2,500. Nevertheless, Waltz's program was more successful than those devised by Clowes and Huffman, since he exploited the need for *consistent* labelling of neighbouring junctions. An iterative technique known as *Waltz filtering* or, more generally, as *relaxation* eliminates possible labellings of junctions, using this consistency constraint. In most cases it rapidly converges on a solution to the segmentation problem for the image it is processing.

Steve Draper (1981) and others have identified a number of problems with the junction-labelling technique and with an alternative to it known as the gradient-space method. Draper invented a technique called *sidedness reasoning*. Sidedness reasoning is about whether two points or surfaces are on the same side of a third surface. Draper showed that this technique was able to segment all BLOCKSWORLD images but in doing so he virtually put a stop to work on object recognition in the BLOCKSWORLD. The reason was that his technique wore on its sleeve the fact that it was specific to BLOCKSWORLD: it works only when all surfaces are flat. Thus, the idea of solving the problem of object recognition in a miniature domain and scaling up the solution to the real world would not work.

A quite different approach to the problems of vision is found in the work of David Marr (1982) and his associates. Marr's work integrates ideas from AI, psychology, and neurophysiology in what is usually taken to be the paradigmatically successful piece of research in cognitive science. The work is guided by an underlying philosophy about the study of natural information-processing systems. Marr identified three levels at which such systems should be studied. First, a *task analysis* answers the questions of what the system does and why it does it. This analysis leads to a *computational theory* of the system – an account of the function (in the mathematical sense) it computes. The second level of analysis is that of *representation and algorithm*. The third level is that of implementation. In the case of natural information processing systems, this level of analysis requires the study of the neural mechanisms that support the system. Marr is critical of previous AI work on vision, largely because of its focus on the second level of analysis at the expense of the first, to which Marr attached great importance. He is also critical of neurophysiological work, such as that of Hubel and Wiesel (1962), in which the purpose of certain types of cell is inferred from their properties. According to Marr, the purpose of a system (and of its parts) can be determined only by constructing a computational theory.

In his own work, Marr recognized three main stages of visual processing. In the first of these stages, the array of light falling on the retina is transformed into a representation called the *primal sketch*. The primal sketch is a symbolic representation, but it is a representation of the image, not of the scene. It contains information about lines, boundaries, and regions in the image. The construction of the primal sketch takes place very early in the visual system and proceeds on the basis of local interactions between processing units (cells) that represent adjacent parts of the image. Although these interactions reflect what is known about the early visual system, Marr eschewed theories what were motivated *solely* by neurophysiological evidence. Hence, his demand for independent support − from task analysis and psychological evidence − for the algorithm and representation he proposed.

In the second stage of visual processing, the $2\frac{1}{2}$ D sketch is derived from the primal sketch. This sketch is a very short-term memory store into which a set of processes writes information about the surfaces (in the scene) represented in the image, their orientation, and their approximate distance from the viewer: the third dimension is not properly represented, hence $2\frac{1}{2}$ D sketch. The most important of these processes are stereopsis, structure from motion, and shape from shading.

Since objects have not yet been recognized, surfaces cannot be identified by reference to information about the objects of which they are part. This aspect of the construction of the $2\frac{1}{2}$ D sketch reflects Marr's preference for *bottom-up* (data-driven) theories of visual processing. The only world knowledge that such theories can claim the visual system uses is a set of general principles, such as that very few points in an image correspond to abrupt changes in the surface represented. Specific information about the scene being viewed is not yet available.

In the final stage of visual processing, a *3D model description* is constructed from the $2\frac{1}{2}$ D sketch. This representation contains information about the identity and three-dimensional structure of the objects in the scene. Marr's account of this final stage is highly speculative, and less closely linked with the psychological and neurophysiological evidence. Marr's basic idea is that objects can be represented, in a *catalogue* stored in long-term memory, as jointed *generalized cylinders* (cylinders whose cross-section changes along their length). The principal axes of these cylinders make up stick figures of the objects represented. He showed that, subject to certain constraints, generalized cylinder representations could be derived from the $2\frac{1}{2}$ D sketch, and then compared with entries in the catalogue, with any necessary rotation and bending at the joints. In practice this matching is difficult, and Marr suggested a process of gradual refinement in the match between the image and the stored representations in the catalogue. This kind of process can be (relatively) time-consuming, and was rejected by Marr in his analyses of the lower levels of visual processing.

Marr's work incorporates, in addition to traditional AI-style programming, much straightforward mathematics. Subsequent work on vision, both theoretical and applied, has become increasingly mathematical and, hence, increasingly inaccessible to psychologists. On the theoretical side, many of the problems of visual analysis have been identified as special cases of what are known as *ill-posed* problems. They are ill posed because, as they stand, they do not have a unique solution. They can be analysed by a technique known as *regularization*, which requires the addition to the problem of the kind of general constraints identified by Marr. On the applied side, specialized hardware in the form of very large-scale integration (VLSI) chips has allowed, for example, stereo algorithms to be used in real-world applications.

THINKING, REASONING, PROBLEM SOLVING

Historically, problem solving was one of the earliest topics of AI research. Furthermore, it has often been argued that it is the central topic, since AI techniques in other domains can be seen as special cases of searching through a "space" of possibilities for a solution to a problem. For example, parsing a sentence can be seen as a search through the (infinite) set of possible syntactic structures defined by the grammar of a language.

Occasionally it is possible to examine all possible solutions to a problem to find the right one. However, for most interesting problems there are too many possibilities to make this approach viable. Usually there are several steps in the solution to a problem, so the number of possible moves multiplies up at each step, producing what is called a *combinatorial explosion* in the number of potential solutions. A *control strategy* for searching through the space of possible solutions is, therefore, required.

Traditionally, there are two ways of representing problems so that a search can be made for their solution. In a *state-space representation*, problems are represented in terms of states of the relevant part of the world, and actions (usually referred to as *operators*) that transform one state into another. In this representation, a single path through the tree of possibilities (= a sequence of operators) represents the solution to the problem. In a *problem-reduction* representation a large problem is broken up into a number of sub-problems, all of which must be solved if the main problem is to be solved. State-space representations are easier to construct. Sensible reductions of problems can be hard to find, but they are very useful when they have been found. In serious AI work on problem solving the two types of representation are combined into AND/OR trees. AND branchings represent problem reductions, where all the sub-goals have to be fulfilled. OR branchings represent alternative possibilities in a state space, only one of which has to be fulfilled.

Various general control strategies for searching problem spaces have been proposed. The most fundamental distinction is between *breadth-first* and *depth-first* search of trees. In breadth-first search all possible one-operator solutions are checked, then all possible two-operator solutions, and so on. In depth-first search one possible solution is followed up until it succeeds or fails, or until a pre-set depth limit is reached, since a branch in an AND/OR tree may never terminate. Simple depth-first and breadth-first search are used only in desperation. Usually some method is introduced for following up the most promising possibilities. Methods for deciding which possibility is the most promising are inevitably heuristic. The most sophisticated method of making the choice is the AO^* algorithm. However, the algorithm itself does not provide the means of measuring which next move is the best. Furthermore, there is no general method for assigning values to moves. A new one must be devised for each domain in which the algorithm is used.

Such methods can, nevertheless, be applied to solving puzzle-book problems and in game-playing computers (e.g., for chess). In chess-playing programs the problem that the computer is trying to solve is not how to win the game, but what move to make next. Successful programs run on very fast super-computers, so that they can examine vast numbers of possible moves. However, they limit the distance ahead (in terms of moves) that they look. Since they typically cannot see ahead to a winning position, they have to evaluate the positions that they can reach in other ways, and then aim to reach the best position that a rational opponent will let them. The play of such programs differs in several ways from that of human chess players. The standard of the best of them, however, is usually reckoned to be in the grandmaster category.

Even if all AI researchers had access to the kind of super-computers that chess programmers use, they would not necessarily want to use the same kind of brute force problem solving methods, particularly if they were interested in modelling human problem solving abilities. Newell, Shaw, and Simon (1957) first introduced the idea of heuristic (rule-of-thumb) problem solving techniques in their Logic Theory Machine, that proved theorems of logic. An alternative way of speeding up problem solving is to use domain-specific techniques, that may be heuristic, but which need not be. An early example of an AI program that used a domain-specific technique was Gelernter's (1963) Geometry Machine, which constructed the equivalent of geometrical diagrams. It is thought that most human mathematicians, except when they are working in completely new areas of mathematics, use domain-specific techniques. More generally, domain-specific techniques are thought to be widely used in all types of problem solving.

LANGUAGE

There is a long history of computational research on all aspects of language processing. Research on speech, both automatic speech recognition and speech synthesis, has been strongly influenced by work on signal processing carried out by electronic engineers. More recently, with the advent of larger and more powerful computers, the field of *speech and language technology* has emerged, which is primarily directed to producing tools for processing large corpora of linguistic data held on computers. Some of the techniques developed may be of interest to AI researchers; others are used to derive statistical information that is of primary interest to, say, lexicographers.

Work on language processing is divided into three parts, concerned respectively with recognizing or selecting words, computing or generating sentence structure, and processing meaning at the level of discourse. Until the 1970s AI research on language processing often produced working systems that understood a substantial portion of a language such as English. Winograd's (1972) SHRDLU, a program that talks about moving blocks around the BLOCKSWORLD, represents the apotheosis of this work. However, it has since become obvious that the component parts of language processing are each so complex that they must be studied separately, if real progress is to be made.

Recent work on word identification has been largely dominated by neural network modelling, in particular the TRACE model of auditory word identification (McClelland & Elman, 1986) and Seidenberg and McClelland's (1989) model of visual word identification. The TRACE model is "hand-coded". It does not use distributed representations, and hence its mode of operation is easy to discern. It has interacting banks of detectors at three levels: for the auditory features of sounds, for phonemes (sounds that correspond roughly to letters), and for words. The Seidenberg and McClelland model, on the other hand, is a model that learns. One of its most interesting features is its eschewal of lexical representations: all its knowledge is encoded in links between orthographic and phonological features.

Investigations of the computation of sentence structure (parsing) have taken two rather different directions. On the one hand, *computational linguists* worry about problems such as the linguistic niceties of describing sentence structure and the computational properties of the procedures that derive the structure for a particular sentence, given a description of how sentences in its language can be structured (a grammar). One of the most important developments in computational models of parsing is the introduction of unification-based approaches (e.g., Kay, 1985). Unification is a technique that is widely used in other branches of AI, in particular theorem proving. Unification-based parsers, like some other parsers, such as chart parsers, have the additional advantage of clearly separating information about how sentences can be structured (the grammar) from information about how sentence structure is computed (the parsing algorithm). In contrast with researchers whose primary interest is in the computational properties of parsing systems, those who attempt to model the way that people derive sentence structure have to take account of well-established empirical findings on, in particular, what happens when people encounter a syntactic ambiguity. It is not yet clear how these two approaches to parsing can be integrated.

Understanding and generating discourse still remain formidable tasks. AI research has often been hampered by a restricted or ad-hoc approach to word meanings. One hope is that linguistically more sophisticated approaches to word meaning, such as Jackendoff's (1990) conceptual semantics, will be taken up by AI researchers. At the level of sentence meaning, AI researchers, at last, agree about the importance of compositional semantics of a broadly Montagovian kind (Dowty, Wall, & Peters, 1981). However, the major problems in describing discourse level processing, which have been known for many years, still resist satisfactory analysis. Some of the most important are figurative and indirect uses of language, coherence, ellipsis, and the role of the other participants' beliefs.

LEARNING

For historical reasons, learning has been a comparatively neglected topic in AI. The information processing approach to understanding intelligent behaviour was seen as a radical alternative to the behaviourism that had dominated psychology, and which placed a strong emphasis on learning. Furthermore, traditional AI aimed to study intelligence at an abstract level, independent of both its genesis (learned or programmed) and its underlying mechanism (carbon or silicon). The study of learning has come back into its own with the increasing importance of connectionist modelling. Nevertheless, a number of important studies of learning have been carried out in the symbolic framework, and the diversity of the learning mechanisms that they investigate contrasts sharply with the behaviourist approach.

Learning by being told often involves little more than adding a fact to a database. However, more abstract pieces of information, such as advice on the best strategy for winning a game, may need to be *operationalized*.

A more complex kind of learning is learning from mistakes. Gerald Sussman's (1975) program HACKER writes its own mini-programs for solving problems of stacking and unstacking blocks in BLOCKSWORLD. However, it can learn only when it can almost solve a problem, and its performance is crucially dependent on its having a "teacher" who presents it with a suitably graded set of problems. Patrick Winston's (1975) program that learns concepts for configurations of blocks (such as arches) in BLOCKSWORLD, similarly learns from almost correct information. When told that something is not quite an arch, it can use that information to deduce what distinguishes arches from non-arches.

As well as recognizing the importance of being almost correct, Winston also emphasized that an important aspect of learning is what is sometimes called *induction* − going beyond the information embodied in the examples presented to the program to form general concepts (in his case) or rules. Positive instances suggest generalizations of the concept or rule, negative instances suggest specializations (or restrictions). Research subsequent to

Winston's, particularly that of Ryszard Michalski (e.g., 1983) has systematized the study of induction, and shown that it can be regarded as a special case of search, with the search space being the set of possible generalizations statable in a particular language. Michalski's approach is more powerful than Winston's, but less closely related to human learning. It can also be used for the related task of discrimination learning. Its disadvantage is that it works straightforwardly only if the generalizations are formulated using exactly the same predicates that are used to describe the instances.

Winston's program can learn more complex concepts (such as arch) only because it knows simpler concepts (pillar, lintel). This aspect of the program relates, very crudely, to the question of how much of what we know about language is learned, and how much is innate. In the case of concepts, it has been argued (e.g., by Fodor, 1981) that all concepts must be innate. More generally, it is widely, though not universally, believed that many general principles governing the form of possible languages are innate, and that the availability of these principles to the language learning mechanism explains how it is able to achieve what appears, on mathematical analysis, to be a difficult or impossible task.

Another famous example of learning by generalization is Arthur Samuel's (1963) checkers (draughts) program. This program develops a general method for evaluating board positions by comparing computed evaluations with the way the game actually turns out, and revising, if necessary, the method of evaluation.

A more ambitious, and more controversial, attempt to study a different kind of learning – learning by exploration – is found in Doug Lenat's (1982) AM (Automated Mathematician) and EURISKO programs. AM starts with a collection of set-theoretic concepts and ways of combining them, and creates further mathematical concepts from them (e.g., positive whole number, prime number, the fundamental theorem of arithmetic – that every number can be expressed as a product of prime factors).

None of the programs described so far provides a convincing model of human learning. People can learn things very quickly, though they often make mistakes in doing so. This very quick learning depends on particular ways of using background knowledge. Two lines of research that attempt to model this kind of learning investigate analogy-based learning and explanation-based learning. The importance of analogy in learning and problem-solving has long been recognized in cognitive psychology. None the less the underlying processes are difficult to model computationally, not least because the domain from which an analogy is drawn need not be specified in advance. In explanation-based learning (see e.g., de Jong, 1988) a single event or episode is explained on the basis of a theory about the relevant aspects of the world. That explanation is then generalized so that it will be useful in other situations.

Traditional AI work on learning has embodied a variety of ideas. An alternative tradition, running from the British Empiricist philosophers of the seventeenth and eighteenth centuries to the behaviourists and neo-behaviourists of the twentieth century, has seen all learning as the formation and strengthening of associations between ideas. In a modified form, this notion also underlies recent connectionist accounts of learning. Connectionists machines are collections of simple processing units, with levels of

OUTPUT

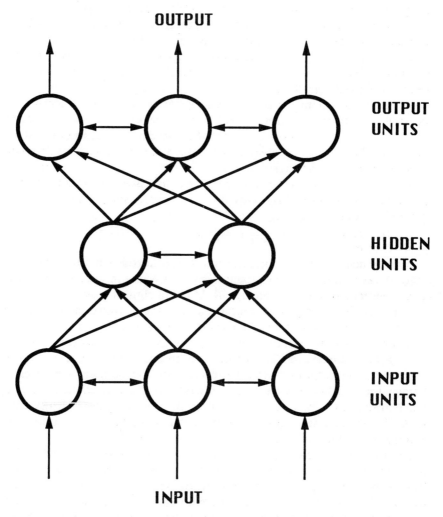

Figure 2 A simple connectionist network showing the three types of unit – input, hidden, and output – and the connections between them

activation that can be passed from one unit to another. A typical machine has three layers of units: input units, hidden units and output units (see Figure 2). Such machines can learn in several ways, but the most popular is known as a *back propagation*. It is a supervised learning method in which a stimulus is encoded at the input units and produces an output at the output units. The supervisor tells the machine what the output should have been, and the difference between the actual and expected outputs is propagated back through the network of units, and used, in a precisely specified way, to adjust the (associative) strengths of the connections between them. Adjustments are small, because the machine must not produce the correct response to the last input at the expense of responding grossly incorrectly to other inputs. Learning is slow, sometimes very slow, but a stable set of associative strengths is usually reached.

Another biological metaphor that has inspired AI work on learning is *evolution. Genetic algorithms* (e.g. Goldberg, 1989) use complex rules to perform tasks. The parts of these rules can be recombined by processes that are analogous to the genetic operations that take place in the germ cells during sexual reproduction. The resulting rules are then allowed to perform their task for some time, and their performance is assessed. Those that do best re-enter the "reproductive" process.

APPLICATIONS

Intelligent machines should be of more than academic interest. However, most of the machines that we interact with in everyday life, for example automatic bank tellers, are not intelligent. More intelligent machines – often referred to as expert systems – do have applications. However, despite the hopes of the early 1980s, it now appears that expert systems will typically be used to assist experts, rather than to replace them. Perhaps the most important area of application for intelligent programs is in medical diagnosis, though there are obviously ethical problems in this domain. One area in which computers play a crucial role is in modern scanning techniques (CAT, PET, NMR, etc.). The basic use of computers in scanning is to generate appropriate images. Intelligent programs might also help to produce diagnoses from images.

One of the earliest, and best known, medical diagnosis systems is MYCIN (Shortliffe, 1976), which diagnoses serious bacterial infections so that life-saving antibiotic drugs can be administered before a culture has been developed. The development of such a system requires the gleaning of information about the diseases in question and their symptoms. Some of this information is elicited from experts, sometimes with difficulty, as the experts cannot necessarily verbalize their knowledge. TEIRESIAS (Davis, 1982) is a program that attempts to automate this knowledge transfer, and also to use the knowledge already in MYCIN to generate user-friendly explanations of its diagnoses. Other diagnostic information comes from statistical records. In an expert system all the information is usually represented in a uniform way, so that new information can readily be added. The rules for making inferences are stored separately, and an attempt is made to keep the inferential processes simple. One of the major aspects of inference in expert systems is combining uncertain bits of information to produce a best guess, for example at a diagnosis. This combination is sometimes achieved using standard statistical (Bayesian) techniques and sometimes using domain specific rules, as in MYCIN (see above).

MYCIN also formed the basis of the first *expert system shell*, E-MYCIN, which is MYCIN stripped of its domain-specific knowledge. Expert system shells were the first of several attempts to make the creation of new expert systems easy. Success has been partial. E-MYCIN, for example, is most successful in other medical diagnosis systems, such as PUFF, which diagnoses pulmonary diseases.

Another well-known expert system is DENDRAL (Lindsay, Buchanan, Feigenbaum, & Lederberg, 1980), which works out the molecular structure of large organic molecules from their mass spectrograms. DENDRAL has been in regular use by research chemists for some time. An additional program, meta-DENDRAL, attempts to formulate new rules using the induction techniques described above.

A second area in which AI has sought to find application is in computer-assisted learning (CAL). With the expansion of higher education in the UK, CAL is likely to become increasingly important, though it is as yet unclear what the contribution of AI techniques will be. The current focus of attention is on multimedia, and in particular hypermedia learning tools, which provide facilities for exploring large databases in various ways, but which rely on much of the intelligence resting in the instructions and with the student.

The intelligent tutoring systems of AI, on the other hand, try to be intelligent themselves. Such systems have three main components: a knowledge base which could, in principle, incorporate multimedia options, a model of the student, and a set of teaching strategies. The knowledge base is used to impart information directly to students, but it is also used to generate explanations of why students' answers to questions are wrong. This process, in turn, makes use of the model of the student to decide what kinds of misconceptions students will have. Such indirect methods of teaching meet with some success, but they prove comparatively difficult to implement in a tutoring system.

PHILOSOPHICAL ISSUES

AI research, more than that in other sciences, has been surrounded by philosophical controversy. Two related issues have provided the major focus

of debate. The first is whether machines can think, and the second is what role they should be allowed to play in our lives.

The question of whether machines can think, although one that excites the popular imagination, is not necessarily a clear one. One crucial aspect of it, however, is whether there is a difference between computer programs that model phenomena such as the weather, which simulate processes in the world, but do not reproduce them, and AI programs. In other words: is a computer running such a program really intelligent, or is it just simulating intelligent behaviour? On one view, most programs lack real intelligence because they do not interact with the world. The symbols that they manipulate have meaning only because of the way they are interpreted by their programmers. On this view a robot that based its interactions with the world on its internal computations could be intelligent. An opposing view is that real intelligence can be manifest only in biological systems (Searle, 1980). To support this thesis Searle put forward his famous *Chinese room* argument. If he sat in a room manipulating symbols according to the rules embodied in a computer program, he might, from the outside, be described as reading and answering questions in Chinese. He would not, however, understand Chinese. So, understanding Chinese is not just running a program. However, Searle's view of what else it is, basically being a biological intelligence, appears to have no foundation, and has been dubbed *protoplasm chauvinism* (Torrance, 1986).

If machines, or at least robots, can be intelligent, we might at some time in the future have moral responsibilities towards them, or we might be in danger of being dominated by them. To some extent the moral issues raised by such considerations are just those that arise in the application of any science. The difference is that we might be faced not simply with a substance or technique that might be misused, but with something that is itself an "alien" intelligence. However, it is difficult to pinpoint, as Weizenbaum (1976) has tried to do, the sense in which intelligent computers pose a special threat.

ARTIFICIAL INTELLIGENCE, COGNITIVE PSYCHOLOGY, AND THE FUTURE

Since the mid-1970s there has been an enormous growth in AI research. It is no longer possible, as it once was, for an AI researcher, let alone a psychologist, to keep up with developments in all of its subfields. Furthermore, much of AI has become very technical: much more so than cognitive psychology. Nevertheless, the best science often is technical; if cognitive psychologists are not to risk being usurped, they should keep at least one eye on developments in AI.

FURTHER READING

Boden, M. A. (1987). *Artificial intelligence and natural man*, 2nd edn. London: MIT Press.

Garnham, A. (1988). *Introduction to artificial intelligence*. London: Routledge.

Garnham, A. (1991). *The mind in action*. London: Routledge.

Rich, E., & Knight, K. (1991). *Artificial intelligence*, 2nd edn. New York: McGraw-Hill.

REFERENCES

Clowes, M. B. (1971). On seeing things. *Artificial Intelligence, 21,* 79–116.

Davis, R. (1982). TEIRESIAS: Applications of meta-level knowledge. In R. Davis & D. Lenat (Eds) *Knowledge-based systems in artificial intelligence* (pp. 227–490). New York: McGraw-Hill.

de Jong, G. (1988). An introduction to explanation-based learning. In H. E. Shrobe (Ed.) *Exploring artificial intelligence: Survey talks from the national conferences on artificial intelligence* (pp. 45–81). San Mateo, CA: Morgan Kaufmann.

Dowty, D. R., Wall, R., & Peters, P. S. (1981). *Introduction to Montague semantics*. Dordrecht: Reidel.

Doyle, J. (1979). A truth maintenance system. *Artificial Intelligence, 12,* 231–272.

Draper, S. W. (1981). The use of gradient and dual space in line-drawing interpretation. *Artificial Intelligence, 17,* 461–508.

Fahlman, S. E. (1979). *NETL: A system for representing and using real-word knowledge*. Cambridge, MA: MIT Press.

Fodor, J. A. (1981). The present status of the innateness controversy. In J. A. Fodor, *Representations* (pp. 257–316). Brighton: Harvester.

Gelernter, H. L. (1963). Realization of a geometry-theorem proving machine. In E. A. Feigenbaum & J. Feldman (Eds) *Computers and thought* (pp. 134–152). New York: McGraw-Hill.

Goldberg, D. (1989). *Genetic algorithms in search, optimization, and machine learning*. Reading, MA: Addison-Wesley.

Guzman, A. (1968). Decomposition of a visual scene into three-dimensional bodies. *Proceedings of the American Federation of Information Processing Studies Fall Joint Conference, 33,* 291–304.

Hubel, D. H., & Wiesel, T. N. (1962). Receptive fields, binocular interaction and functional architecture in the cat's visual cortex. *Journal of Physiology, 160,* 106–154.

Huffman, D. A. (1971). Impossible objects as nonsense sentences. In B. A. Meltzer & D. Michie (Eds) *Machine intelligence 6* (pp. 295–323). Edinburgh: Edinburgh University Press.

Jackendoff, R. S. (1990). *Semantic structures*. Cambridge, MA: MIT Press.

Kay, M. (1985). Parsing in functional unification grammar. In D. R. Dowty, L. Karttunen, & A. M. Zwicky (Eds) *Natural language parsing: Psychological, computational, and theoretical perspectives*. (pp. 251–278). Cambridge: Cambridge University Press.

Lenat, D. M. (1982). AM: Discovery in mathematics as heuristic search. In R. Davis & D. M. Lenat (Eds) *Knowledge-based systems in artificial intelligence* (pp. 1–225). New York: McGraw-Hill.

Lighthill, J. (1972). *Artificial intelligence: Report to the Science Research Council*. London: Science Research Council.

Lindsay, R., Buchanan, B. G., Feigenbaum, E. A., & Lederberg, J. (1980). *Applications of artificial intelligence for chemical inference: The DENDRAL project*. New York: McGraw-Hill.

McClelland, J. L., & Elman, J. L. (1986). The TRACE model of speech perception. *Cognitive Psychology, 18*, 1–86.

Marr, D. (1982). *Vision: A computational investigation into the human representation and processing of visual information*. San Francisco, CA: Freeman.

Michalski, R. S. (1983). A theory and methodology of inductive learning. *Artificial Intelligence, 20*, 111–161.

Newell, A., Shaw, J. C., & Simon, H. A. (1957). Empirical explorations with the Logic Theory Machine: A case study in heuristics. *Proceedings of the Western Joint Computer Conference, 15*, 218–230.

Quillian, M. R. (1968). Semantic memory. In M. Minsky (Ed.) *Semantic information processing* (pp. 216–270). Cambridge, MA: Massachusetts Institute of Technology Press.

Robinson, J. A. (1965). A machine-oriented logic based on the resolution principle. *Journal of the Association for Computing Machinery, 12*, 23–41.

Samuel, A. L. (1963). Some studies in machine learning using the game of checkers. In E. A. Feigenbaum & J. Feldman (Eds) *Computers and thought* (pp. 71–105). New York: McGraw-Hill.

Searle, J. R. (1980). Minds, brains, and programs. *Behavioral and Brain Sciences, 3*, 417–424.

Seidenberg, M., & McClelland, J. L. (1989). A distributed, developmental model of word recognition and naming. *Psychological Review, 96*, 523–568.

Shortliffe, E. H. (1976). A model of inexact reasoning in medicine. *Mathematical Biosciences, 23*, 361–379.

Sussman, G. (1975). *A computer model of skill acquisition*. New York: Elsevier.

Torrance, S. (1986). Breaking out of the Chinese room. In M. Yazdani (Ed.) *Artificial intelligence: Principles and applications* (pp. 294–314). London: Chapman & Hall.

Waltz, D. (1975). Understanding line drawings of scenes with shadows. In P. H. Winston (Ed.) *The psychology of computer vision* (pp. 19–92). New York: McGraw-Hill.

Weizenbaum, J. (1976). *Computer power and human reason*. San Francisco, CA: Freeman.

Winograd, T. (1972). Understanding natural language. *Cognitive Psychology, 3*, 1–191.

Winston, P. H. (1975). Learning structural descriptions from examples. In P. H. Winston (Ed.) *The psychology of computer vision* (pp. 155–209). New York: McGraw-Hill.

GLOSSARY

This glossary is confined to a selection of frequently used terms that merit explanation or comment. Its informal definitions are intended as practical guides to meanings and usages. The entries are arranged alphabetically, word by word, and numerals are positioned as though they were spelled out.

afferent neurons from the Latin *ad*, to, *ferre*, to carry, neurons (q.v.) that transmit impulses from the sense organs to the central nervous system (CNS) (q.v.). *Cf.* efferent neurons.

amnesia partial or complete loss of memory (q.v.). Anterograde amnesia is loss of memory for events following the amnesia-causing trauma, or loss of the ability to form long-term memories for new facts and events; retrograde amnesia is loss of memory for events occurring shortly before the trauma.

anterograde amnesia *see* under amnesia.

arousal a general term for an organism's state of physiological activation, mediated by the autonomic nervous system (q.v.). *See also* Yerkes-Dodson law.

articulatory loop a system in working memory or short-term memory (q.v.) that holds and uses inner speech. *Cf.* central executive, visuo-spatial sketchpad.

artificial intelligence (AI) the science of designing machines or computer programs to do things normally done by minds, such as playing chess, thinking logically, writing poetry, composing music, or analysing chemical substances. Largely unconscious functions of intelligence, such as those involved in vision and language, present especially difficult challenges to AI.

autonomic nervous system a subdivision of the nervous system that regulates (autonomously) the internal organs and glands. It is divided into the sympathetic nervous system and the parasympathetic nervous system (qq.v.).

availability heuristic a heuristic (q.v.) in which the frequency or probability of an event is judged by the number of instances of it that can readily be brought to mind and that are thus cognitively available. It can generate biased or incorrect conclusions, as when people are asked whether the English language contains more words beginning with the letter *r* or more with *r* as the third letter. Most people find it easier to think of instances of the former than the latter and so conclude wrongly that there are more words beginning with *r*.

axon from the Greek word meaning axis, a process or extending fibre of a neuron (q.v.) which conducts impulses away from the cell body (q.v.) and transmits them to other neurons.

base rate fallacy a tendency to take insufficient account of the base rates of occurrence of events when making judgements or decisions, as when people are more afraid of having accidents when flying than driving even though the risk of accidents is far higher when driving.

behaviourism a school of psychology founded by John B. Watson in 1913 which considers objectively observed behaviour rather than inner mental experiences to be the proper subject for study. Behaviourists tend to stress the importance of the environment as a determinant of human and animal behaviour.

bottom-up processing in cognitive psychology, information processing that proceeds from 'raw' sensory stimuli and then works up to more abstract cognitive operations, as for example in a computational theory of vision. *Cf.* top-down processing.

cell body sometimes called the *soma*, the central part of a neuron (q.v.), containing the nucleus and other structures that keep the cell alive.

central executive the attentional coordinating system of working memory or short-term memory (q.v.). *Cf.* articulatory loop, visuo-spatial sketchpad.

central nervous system (CNS) in human beings and other vertebrates, the brain and spinal cord.

chunking the tendency to organize small items of information into larger meaningful units or 'chunks' as, for example, when a skilled reader takes in whole words or phrases at a glance without noticing individual letters separately or when an accomplished musical sight reader processes several bars of music as a single chunk.

cognition from the Latin *cognoscere*, to know, attention, thinking, problem-solving, remembering, and all other mental processes that fall under the general heading of information processing.

cognitive neuropsychology one of the major approaches to cognition, in which patterns of normal and impaired functioning in brain-damaged patients is examined with a view to providing information that has a bearing on competing cognitive theories.

cognitive psychology the branch of psychology devoted to the study of attention, memory, imagery, perception, language, thinking, problem solving, artificial intelligence (AI), and generally all mental operations that involve information processing.

cognitive schema (pl. schemata or schemas) an integrated network of knowledge, beliefs and expectations relating to a particular subject; in Piaget's theory of cognitive development, the basic element of mental life.

cognitive science an umbrella term for an interdisciplinary enterprise, involving cognitive psychology, the brain sciences, computer science, artificial intelligence, linguistics, and philosophy, to construct theoretical models of cognition (q.v.).

conjunction fallacy a tendency to judge the joint probability of two events (e.g., Jack is an accountant who plays jazz for a hobby) as greater than the probability of one of its constituent events (Jack plays jazz for a hobby), even though this is logically impossible.

connectionism an approach to artificial intelligence (q.v.) involving the design of intelligent systems composed of groups of interconnected processing units, in which items of knowledge are represented not at single locations but as patterns over collections of units, and these patterns are adaptive inasmuch as they are capable of learning from experience. It is also called parallel distributed processing.

convergent thinking thinking characterized by synthesis of information, especially in the course of arriving at a unique solution to a problem; analytical, usually deductive thinking in which formal rules are followed, as in arithmetic. *Cf.* divergent thinking.

correlation in statistics, the relationship between two variables such that high scores on one tend to go with high scores on the other or (in the case of negative correlation) such that high scores on one tend to go with low scores on the other. The usual

98

index of correlation, called the product-moment correlation coefficient and symbolized by r, ranges from 1.00 for perfect positive correlation, through zero for uncorrelated variables, to -1.00 for perfect negative correlation.

dendrite from the Greek *dendron*, tree, the collection of branched, threadlike extensions of a neuron (q.v.) that receives impulses from other neurons or from a receptor and conducts them towards the cell body.

divergent thinking imaginative thinking characterized by the generation of multiple possible solutions to a problem, often associated with creativity. *Cf.* convergent thinking.

echoic store the sensory memory (q.v.) register or store for auditory information. *Cf.* iconic store.

efferent neurons from the Latin *e*, from, *ferre*, to carry, neurons (q.v.) that transmit impulses away from the central nervous system (CNS) (q.v.) towards the muscles, glands, etc. *Cf.* afferent neurons.

emotion from the Latin *e*, away, *movere*, to move, any evaluative, affective, intentional, short-term psychological state.

episodic memory a type of memory for specific experiences or episodes, generally stored together with information about where and how the information was acquired. *Cf.* semantic memory.

feature detectors sensory neurons that are particularly responsive to specific features of stimuli, for example a line detector, a corner detector, or a voice-onset detector.

flashbulb memory a vivid, detailed, long-term memory (LTM) (q.v.) for the surrounding circumstances in which one experienced or learned about some historical or significant event.

heuristic from the Greek *heuriskein*, to discover, any of a number of methods of solving complex problems by means of rough-and-ready rules of thumb. *See also* availability heuristic, representativeness heuristic.

hippocampus from the Greek *hippos*, horse, *kampos*, sea monster, a structure in the brain, whose cross section has the shape of a sea horse, involved in emotion, motivation, learning, and the establishment of long-term memory.

iconic store from the Latin *icon*, image, the sensory memory register or store for visual information. *Cf.* echoic store. *See also* sensory memory.

interference *see under* proactive interference (PI), retroactive interference (RI).

introspection from the Latin *intro*, towards the inside, *specere*, to look, the act of examining one's own mental experiences.

long-term memory (LTM) relatively long-lasting memory for information that has been deeply processed. *Cf.* sensory memory, short-term memory (STM).

memory the mental processes of encoding, storage, and retrieval of information. *See also* amnesia, episodic memory, flashbulb memory, long-term memory, semantic memory, sensory memory, short-term memory (STM), state-dependent memory.

motivation the driving forces responsible for the initiation, persistence, direction, and vigour of goal-directed behaviour.

nervous system *see under* autonomic nervous system, central nervous system (CNS), parasympathetic nervous system, sympathetic nervous system.

neural network in cognitive science and artificial intelligence, a type of abstract model of knowledge representation, characteristic of connectionism (q.v.).

neuron from the Greek word for nerve, a nerve cell, which is the basic structural and functional unit of the nervous system, consisting of a cell body, axon, and dendrites (qq.v.). See also afferent neuron, efferent neuron.

neurophysiology the study of the operation of the nervous system (q.v.).

nonsense syllables consonant-vowel-consonant trigrams, such as VUD or KEJ, presumed to be relatively meaningless, used in the study of memory.

parallel distributed processing see connectionism.

parasympathetic nervous system one of the two major divisions of the autonomic nervous system; its general function is to conserve metabolic energy. *Cf.* sympathetic nervous system.

PDP parallel distributed processing. *See* connectionism.

phoneme from the Greek *phonema*, a sound, any class of speech sounds regarded in a given language as merely variant pronunciations of the same speech sound.

positivity bias a tendency to seek positive confirmation for hypotheses rather than evidence refuting its negation.

proactive interference (PI) the inhibitory effect of information learned in the past on the learning of new information, especially noticeable when the two sets of material are very similar. *Cf.* retroactive interference (RI).

psychoanalysis a theory of mental structure and function and a method of psychotherapy based on the writings of Sigmund Freud and his followers, focusing primarily on unconscious mental processes and the various defence mechanisms that people use to repress them.

psycholinguistics the psychology of language, including language acquisition in children, the mechanisms underlying adult production and comprehension of language, and language disorders.

psychology from the Greek *psyche*, mind, *logos*, study, the study of the nature, functions, and phenomena of behaviour and mental experience.

receptor a sense organ or structure that is sensitive to a specific form of physical energy and that transmits neural information to other parts of the nervous system.

retroactive interference (RI) the inhibiting effect that the learning of new information has on the recall of material learned previously, especially when the two sets of material are very similar. *Cf.* proactive interference (PI).

representativeness heuristic a heuristic (q.v.) in which judgements tend to be based on the representativeness of an instance rather than any other factors affecting its likelihood, for example when people judge a conservatively dressed man with little interest in politics to be an engineer rather than a lawyer even when they know that he was selected from a group composed of 70 per cent lawyers and only 30 per cent engineers.

retrograde amnesia *See* amnesia.

saccade from the French word meaning a jerk on the reins of a horse, a sudden movement of the eyes from one fixation point to another, such as occurs when reading.

schema *see* cognitive schema.

semantic memory memory for information encoded verbally according to its meaning. *Cf.* episodic memory.

sense organ *see* receptor.

sensory memory, a form of memory, necessary for normal vision and hearing, which allows visual images to be stored for about half a second and sounds for up to two seconds. Sensory memory enables television, which presents 30 still images per second, to convey the illusion of a single moving image. It also makes speech intelligible, because without it, by the end of each spoken word the hearer would have forgotten its beginning. *See also* sensory registers. *Cf.* long-term memory, short term memory.

sensory registers subsystems of sensory memory (q.v.), such as (for vision) the iconic store and (for hearning) the echoic store (qq.v.), generally assumed to exist separately for each sensory modality.

serial position effect a tendency for items that are positioned towards the beginning and end of a list to be remembered better than those in the middle positions.

shadowing a technique for studying attentional processes in which the subject listens to two messages simultaneously and attempts to repeat, or shadow, one of them.

short-term memory (STM) a memory store, also called working memory, consisting of a central executive, visuo-spatial sketchpad, and articulatory loop (qq.v.) that is used for storing small amounts of information for periods of time ranging from a few seconds to a few minutes. It has a severely limited capacity of about seven or eight items of information, such as digits of a telephone number, and the information is rapidly forgotten unless it is refreshed by rehearsal, following which it may eventually be transferred to long-term memory (LTM) (q.v.). *See also* sensory memory.

soma *see* cell body.

state-dependent memory memory for information learned in a particular state of consciousness – for example, in a particular emotional state or under the influence of alcohol or drugs – that can be recalled only when in a similar state. Thus material learned in an intoxicated state is sometimes remembered only in a later intoxicated state, and a person in a depressed state may perhaps be more likely to remember unhappy experiences from the past, which might exacerbate the depression and creates a vicious circle.

subjects from the Latin *sub*, under, *jacere*, to throw, people or other organisms whose behaviour or mental experience is investigated in psychological research.

sympathetic nervous system one of the two major divisions of the autonomic nervous system; it is concerned with general activation, and it mobilizes the body's reaction to stress or perceived danger. *Cf.* parasympathetic nervous system.

tip-of-the-tongue (TOT) phenomenon the frustrating feeling of certainty that a particular name, word, or other item of information is available in long-term memory even though one cannot recall (the whole of) it.

top-down processing in cognitive psychology, information processing that proceeds from general assumptions or presuppositions about the material being processed. *Cf.* bottom-up processing.

unconscious occurring without awareness or intention; in psychoanalysis (q.v.), the name for the part of the mind containing instincts, impulses, images, and ideas of which one is not normally aware.

visuo-spatial sketchpad a system in working memory or short-term memory (q.v.) that is used for setting up and manipulating visual images. **Cf.** articulatory loop, central executive.

working memory *see* short-term memory (STM).

Yerkes-Dodson law a psychological law named after its proposers stating that optimal performance on a variety of tasks occurs at intermediate levels of arousal (q.v.).

INDEX

103